PRECIOUS & PERVERSE

SHORT STORIES

By

Will Wright

Contents

Exploring the Light and Dark sides of Human Nature

THE HEAD 1

BRIEF VISIT 6

STORM OVER DEERHART 10

BEST OF FRIENDS 14

A CURIOUS NIGHT 19

FULL OF HIMSELF 28

SUMMER FUN TRILOGY 31

    I DEAD SUCKER 31

    II SURPRISE PARTY 38

    III THE BEE STING 47

BURTON & THE BULL 56

FOOLING DEATH 61

REFLECTION IN A MOTEL MIRROR 71

TINY TEARS 73

NATURE TAKES ITS COURSE 83

MAN OF HABIT 92

RENNY & SAM 99

WRONG NUMBER 103

COLD WINTER MORNING 110

MAUDE & LYMAN GO SOUTH 115

SPECIAL FAVOR 122

GONE TOO FAR 131

THE ROACH 137

MAUDE & LYMAN GO TO THE AIRPORT 149

THESE THINGS HAPPEN 155

TORTOISE 164

TIME FLIES 170

COFFEE AT THE MIDNIGHT DINER 178

TWO TO TANGO 181

ACKNOWLEDGEMENTS 188

ABOUT THE AUTHOR 189

For Dana

We never learned to tango (my bad), but in this dance of life

we sure can cut a rug!

THE HEAD

Momma told us right from the beginning that it was gonna be an easy birth. I guess she'd know, seeing as how there were already six of us, and she'd had problems with some. I'd come out backward, and Jenny had to be cut out. But with little Eddie, she just smiled and said, "It's gonna be special."

And she was right. Momma never got any bigger than a grapefruit, and when she went into labor, she didn't even call the midwife. "Just get me a clean towel," she said, lying down on her bed and spreading her legs.

We all huddled around expectantly, Poppa included, who held Momma's hand and smiled at her. She gave a little grunt, squeezed his hand and, squoosh, out come this little thing looked like, well, a grapefruit. Only it wasn't really a fruit. As far as we could tell, it was a head with a patch of black hair, eyes, nose, mouth, and ears. Jenny scooped it up in the towel and handed it to Momma, who looked it over like she was inspecting a melon.

"It's a boy," she said, beaming at Poppa. I wasn't quite sure how she knew, except she pointed at a little dangly thing at the back of its skull, just hidden by the hairline. "And quite a handsome one at that!" she added, ruffling the newborn's hair.

We lived in a little farm town in the hills of Vermont, so it was okay that Eddie was a little different because no one saw it that way. He wasn't the only misfit around and ended up being just one of the gang. He matured quickly, even growing some little flippers below each ear so he could propel himself along at a pretty good clip.

He was a rough and tumble little guy and, needless to say, was always pretty dirty. He didn't have to wear any clothes. Couldn't really, nothing to hang onto. And his bottom, which by now had developed into a kind of banana curve from ear to ear, was always coated with a slick layer of dirt, especially during mud season. Momma would snatch him up as soon as he'd roll through the door at sundown and scrub his underside till it was raw. He used to bitch and moan at this, but Momma didn't pay him any mind, saying, "Cleanliness is next to Godliness."

He did have a little fanny slit located where you might think, and she always made sure to clean that real good. He didn't leave much of a business, but he also couldn't clean himself. I think this was the only thing that embarrassed him when we played outside, especially if there were any girls around, which there usually were, somehow attracted to this little fella with the tiny penis always wagging at the back of his head. That, and without hands, he couldn't feed himself, neither. The girls were always trying to give him little treats, and, unfortunately, he started getting plump. Some of the mean boys in town called him Fat Head Ed, and then he would get real pissed. He'd build up a good head of steam, doin' the Thunder Roll, as he called it, and fling himself at some bully's legs like a bowling ball going after some pins. Knocked down a few in his time on this earth, which wasn't that long.

Eddie's only fault was that he was mostly too nice. Maybe it come from being just a head and not having a lot of cards to play, but he'd go out of his way to please just about anyone he could. And he loved to hang out in the schoolyard after the final bell and join in any of the pickup games going on. He really loved sports. I guess it was one area where he felt he could stand out and contribute to the community. We were a poor little village and mostly hard-pressed to afford any decent athletic gear. Eddie figured he could fill a void in this area. I used to try to protect him by protesting if, say, he'd volunteer his services to act as the ball in a soccer game. But I wasn't always there.

2

One day he come home with a big bruise on his side, just under an ear, and Momma cried when he babbled on about "how it was okay that he didn't mind being kicked around, treated like a normal kid."

And football wasn't too bad, long as he survived the punts. He was actually pretty aerodynamic and made a good spiral when passed. And if he was fumbled, he could scoot back to a teammate, usually in time for his team to retain possession. But baseball was another matter.

It was in the spring of Eddie's ninth year. He'd managed to survive all sorts of mishaps and serious physical injury along the way and had won the admiration of most of the kids in town. And I had managed to keep him away from baseball, knowing his love for the game and that his one great desire in life was to become a baseball. I knew, even with my limited knowledge, that he could never survive being struck repeatedly with a bat. But one day, we were out wanting to play, except we couldn't find a ball, and Eddie said he'd be the ball. Even though I wanted to play real bad, I knew this wasn't a good idea and said to everyone, "Let's go home."

All the guys, and some big girls, began to grumble, saying that life sucked if you couldn't even play ball on a nice spring day. That's when Eddie came up with an idea.

"I'll put on the catcher's mask," he said (we had fashioned one out of some heavy-duty chicken wire). "I won't get hurt, least not enough to do much damage."

Everyone thought that was a good idea, and after thinking it over, I even had to agree. He had survived a lot of abuse over the years, what with being kicked, tossed, and dropped, and so on.

Eddie grinned. "As a matter of fact, don't think anyone can hit me."

That brought about a series of catcalls, hoots, hollers, and a bunch of "Gonna smack you good, Eddie," so I guess I finally gave in and yelled, "Play ball!"

As the game progressed, everything was going smoothly. Eddie, not really wanting to get hit with a baseball bat going a hundred miles an hour, deftly manipulated his flippers on the way in from the pitcher's mound to change direction—just before each batter swung and missed. He added new meaning to the "sinker"—called it his "stinker." And his curveball was a thing of beauty.

Both sides had a no-hitter going into the bottom of the ninth with two outs. Sun was going down, visibility getting bad, and guess who come to bat? Me. Everyone was calling for a hit, a homer, to end the game—even the other team. But, heck, I couldn't wallop my own flesh and blood. Eddie came in on the first pitch, and I watched him fly by into the catcher's mitt.

"Strike one!" shouted the umpire.

"C'mon, brother, hit me!" Eddie cried as the catcher tossed him back to the pitcher. "I'm comin' right down the middle!"

The next pitch come in, and Eddie didn't alter his flight pattern one bit.

"Strike two!" shouted the ump.

"Last chance!" Eddie yelled on his way back to the mound.

All the kids chanted, "We wanna hit! We wanna hit!"

4

"It won't hurt but a little," Eddie called in from the pitcher's mound. "Do it!"

The pitcher wound up and tossed Eddie nice and easy. He floated toward me, waist high—the perfect pitch. I swung and *thwack,* made the most solid contact I'd ever made on a ball, or a head for that matter. Eddie took off at the crack of the bat. The catcher's mask split in two and fell away from him like parts of the space shuttle (I seen it on TV).

Everyone turned and watched as he sailed toward left field. Jumping up and down, they yelled, 'Go, Eddie! Go, Eddie!"

I could have sworn I saw his little flippers flappin' in the breeze, helping to propel himself along like a free little bird. He sailed over the fence, hit the ground, and rolled onto the street. A logging truck slammed on its brakes, but too late.

We ran out to the street, many of us hopping the fence, just in time to see the logger, dog-eared John Deere hat in hand, standing over Eddie. We formed a circle around Eddie, who looked like a bloody pancake and a bunch of us wept. We knew he wasn't coming back.

The tarmac was wicked hot from the day's sun, and Eddie shriveled like an egg frying in a skillet without any lard. After about a half hour of weeping and carrying on, the kids headed off. I peeled Eddie off the hot tar and carried him home.

Momma was philosophical about the whole thing, saying Eddie had lived a full life for his young age. She cleaned him up, Poppa put a couple coats of shellac on him, and we've been using him as a hot plate ever since.

BRIEF VISIT

John watched from his rocker on the front porch as the middle-aged man got out of his car. Even with their differences in age, the resemblance was clear—the aristocratic nose, high forehead, and wide-set blue eyes. The curly hair, when John had hair. But when the man stepped onto the porch and held out his hand, John felt a chill. The long slender fingers, those of an artist, a musician, could have been his. He took the hand.

"You must be John," the man said.

John couldn't take his eyes off the man's hand. Nodded.

"I'm Randall," the man said.

John glanced up. "Of course." Then back at the hands. "You have warm hands."

Randall stuck his hand in his coat pocket. "It's chilly out here."

John gazed at the sun rising over the snow-capped mountain peak across the valley. "It'll warm up."

"I can't stay long. Plane to catch," Randall said.

"Where do you live?" John said.

"Oakland."

"That makes sense." John studied the worn planks under his feet. "How did you find me?"

"Google."

"Google?"

"Internet."

"I've heard of the Internet."

Randall sat down in a rocker next to John. They both stared out across the road at the dense pinewoods.

"It's been forty years. What took you so long?" John said.

"Mother didn't tell me your name until the day before she died."

"I'd forgotten hers until your phone call," John said. "Not that I hadn't tried to remember over the years. Cynthia. She was special."

Randall scoffed. "And that's why you left her?"

"I had no idea. Besides, we were never together. I met her the night I was leaving town."

"The night you fucked her in a closet?"

John reached to take Randall's hand, but Randall pulled away.

"It wasn't like that," John said.

"What was it 'like' then? Wait. I don't want to know." Randall stood up.

"It was a magical encounter—a joining of two loving spirits. That's about as good as I can put it."

Randall slumped back down in his rocker. "Mother told me you were a sweet man. She made you sound like a Prince Charming."

John laughed. "I was on my way to New York City to seek my fortune, so to speak. There was a party. I saw your mother sitting alone. We didn't know each other, but our eyes met, and I went over to her. We had a quiet conversation. I'll never forget her eyes, soft and inviting. In fact, everything about her was soft and inviting. I think we knew right away that we were going to make love. We found a walk-in closet, plenty big—"

"I don't need any details."

"Of course."

Randall looked at his watch. "I have to go."

John sat motionless.

Randall stood and held out his hand.

John took it. "You have my hands. Are you an artist, as well?"

"I play the violin."

John clapped his hands. "Wonderful! Your mother and I … melted together. I'm not surprised we conceived. I'll never forget her."

"You couldn't remember her name."

"But I've remembered that night, the feeling, after all these years."

Randall walked down the porch steps.

"Will you come again?" John said.

Randall paused and took in the mountains, then got in his car and waved as he drove off.

STORM OVER DEERHART

My father worked in a Midwest foundry. In summer, the temperature around the furnaces got so intolerable he'd come home looking like a baked potato. My little sis and I always liked this time of year because we knew it wouldn't be long before he'd shuffle up the three flights to our city apartment and, drenched in sweat, collapse on the couch and say, "Pack your bags."

The resort was situated on Deerhart Lake, just outside the town named after it. The lake was small enough that you could stand on the dock of our guest cottage, one of many, and see around the entire shoreline. Even hear Mr. Jones on the far side yelling at his barking dog to shut up. We kids loved to paddle the rowboat, dragging our fishing lines to hook a sunfish or, if we got lucky, get an invitation from old Mrs. Duffin to stop off at her pier for some ice-cold lemonade. And we'd swim in the warm water until our skin shriveled like dried prunes.

The resort's centerpiece was the big hotel. Its shadow at sundown stretched halfway across the water. You could play ping-pong on the wrap-around porch, shuffleboard and horseshoes on the lawn down below, and there were six tennis courts. There was always a big turnout for Thursday night Bingo.

For us kids, the best part of the hotel's Wednesday night barbeque was hunting bullfrogs by flashlight. Our homemade gigs had tines of razor-sharp sixteen-penny nails (sis was quick and not squeamish at all). The adults drank lots of beer and stuffed themselves with beer-soaked bratwurst. They would cheer when we came up from the creek with a bagful of fat croakers, father grilling their plump legs to perfection.

But the highlight of our yearly vacation was having breakfast at the hotel, which we did as a treat once or twice during our stay. The proprietors, George and Mindy Gruber, who had owned the hotel for over forty years, served breakfast to the fifty guests the dining room held.

Over the years, we had observed something peculiar about the Grubers. They seemed to behave like the weather. On a sunny day, they were all smiles and laughter, flitting about like butterflies pouring juice and coffee and passing out extra "best in the world sausage" without even being asked. When it was overcast, they lurked behind your table, silent and foreboding, waiting for you to finish so that they could seat new guests. And if it was raining with a chance of a thunderstorm, you considered playing sick so you wouldn't have to suffer through a harrowing experience. But I could never give up my sausage.

On this particular morning, there was a steady rain with ominous clouds growing darker by the minute. Mother and Father had to bribe us with the promise of cotton candy before we'd get out of bed.

The four of us eased into the dining room and slid into the first open table. It was near an exit, which made me feel a little better. Outside, the wind was picking up, the now torrential rain pelting the windows. Mindy Gruber, the normally tight bun on the back of her head askew, raced up to our table and splashed water from a pitcher in the general direction of our glasses.

"Ready to order?" she puffed.

"Yes," Father said, "I'd—"

She flew off, spilling water on unsuspecting guests before disappearing into the kitchen.

George Gruber burst through the swinging kitchen door, a huge platter balanced over his head. Mindy followed with a stainless cart loaded with scrambled eggs, French toast, muffins, and fruit bowls. George stood in the middle of the room. "Get your red hots here!" he yelled, tossing sausages like footballs to our outstretched hands. I made a handsome leaping catch. Mindy, with one foot on the back rail of her cart, propelled herself around scooter-like, dumping globs of food on tables.

A bolt of lightning flashed across the sky. George and Mindy froze in mid-action. Our family knew the drill and dove under the table. All the regulars did the same. Newcomers looked puzzled.

I counted the seconds until a peal of thunder in the distance rattled the enormous chandelier, making a pretty tinkling sound.

George dropped his platter, and Mindy, with a swift kick, sent her cart crashing into a wall. I watched wide-eyed as they turned to each other and, thrusting out their chests, stretched to their full heights—tall and proud as two short and stout people could be.

A streak of lightning reflected off George's sweaty bald head. A moment later, a loud rumble, closer now, shook the building.

Looking into each other's eyes, they held hands and then, gazing toward the heavens, belted out, as I was to discover later, a verse from Wagner's, The Ride of The Valkyries.

Valkyries, ride over the battlefield.

I'm dying and glad to bleed ...

The harmony on "glad to bleed" was so off-key it made my teeth chatter.

12

Because I know today, I will take my place

With the heroes in Valhalla of old ...

When they hit the ear-piercing "old," lightning flashed, and overhead, in chorus, thunder KA-BOOMED! The foundation rocked. Windows shattered. People screamed and cried out like babies as they crawled toward the exits. George and Mindy swooned and fell in a heap.

And just like that, the sun came out. The birds began to sing. People stopped whimpering and peeked out from under their tables. Those near the exits brushed broken glass from their knees. George and Mindy rose up, entwined like morning glories greeting the day. Faces flushed, they broke into a big smile and opened their mouths to sing. Everyone ducked for cover.

"Just kidding!" they shouted, skipping off hand in hand toward the kitchen, whistling a popular polka tune of the day.

The next day, taking note of scattered showers in the forecast, we skipped breakfast at the hotel and went into the village to watch the annual Road Race—the real reason father liked coming to the lake. Finely tuned sports cars zoomed through the spectator-lined streets. One skidded around a sharp turn and, as it whizzed past, brushed against the hay bale, protecting sis and me as we picked away at our cotton candy.

BEST OF FRIENDS

I would like to tell you a story about my best friend. Let's call him Rob to protect the innocent. Although he never achieved any real fame, he deserved it. In my eyes, he was a remarkable man. He lived a rich and varied life, was immensely creative, dedicated to hard work, and wanted to be nothing but the best in whatever he did. He died a tortured soul, although, in my mind, he was very courageous. I am telling you this story because I don't want him to be forgotten.

I met Rob at a New England boarding school. I was there on a full academic scholarship. I was very smart, and my family was very poor. As part of my scholarship, I had to spend four years on kitchen duty, prepping for meals. I got very good at sharpening knives. Rob was there because his ancestors had endowed the school with a large sum of money, and his father had built the basketball auditorium. He excelled in several sports and never had any problem getting the girls. I, as you have probably surmised, was, and still am, a nerd. I was the basketball team manager (I loved doing the stats), and for some reason Rob took a liking to me. I didn't have a lot of friends, so I was overjoyed with his attention.

We formed an odd couple, and I asked him from time to time why he liked me. He'd pat me on the shoulder and say, "Because we're different. You use your brain. I use my dick." Then he'd laugh. For one so talented, he had a self-deprecating sense of humor. I forgot to mention that he started playing guitar in sophomore year and became proficient right away. He was also a fine artist. But I always beat him in chess.

We both went off to separate colleges and only saw each other during vacations. When we got together, we would share our experiences. Mine, few and shallow, mostly having to do with academics. His, bold and adventurous, having to do with conquests of the opposite sex or some mountain he had climbed. He had taken up golf, made the team, and thought of turning pro. He liked the game because it finally made him think as well as control his emotions. I told him he was heading in the right direction. He smiled at me.

After college, I got a job at an accounting firm. Backed by his father, Rob spent four years on a golf mini-tour. He called me up one day and said he had quit because he had "hit a wall." Couldn't better his plus-two handicap. He was also tired of living off his father's money and wanted to make it on his own. He moved to the Bay Area and became a carpenter, much to his parent's horror.

A few years later, we met up in San Francisco. It was in the sixties. He was a different person. I was the same old me. He had long hair, was playing the sitar, and had dropped acid. He told me he had seen the "light" and was convinced that he was destined to become a great spiritual leader. He meditated for four hours a day. He asked me to try it, but I couldn't sit still for more than a few minutes. He was understanding, though, and said that the world would always need someone to add and subtract numbers. He laughed. I wasn't happy with this comment and let him know. He said that he was serious. That he admired me because I was "solid." No surprises. Someone he could always count on to ground him when he got lost in the "illusory nature of the universe." I didn't understand what he meant, but it sounded good. Our friendship was more important than quibbling over philosophy, or lack thereof. He started a small ashram and had a strong following of devotees. But, as with most things with Rob, after a few years, he gave it up. He told me that he would never be enlightened in this lifetime, that it wasn't his "karma." He seemed pretty enlightened to me, a peaceful person. But what did I know?

All along, he had continued to play the guitar and, after tiring of singing devotional songs to Krishna, decided that he would become a great classical guitarist. Go for it, I told him. You do everything well. To make a living, he began teaching guitar while he was taking classical guitar lessons. After leaving the golf tour, he told his parents that he wanted no support from them, and that he wanted to make it on his own. His father told him to do whatever, that he would never have to worry, regardless of his success or non-success. There was a lot of money coming to him when he, his father, died. Rob didn't want to be rich. He was tired of that. He wanted to suffer like ninety-nine-point-nine percent of the rest of the world. The classical guitar lasted seven years. He became an accomplished performer and even made a couple of albums. But then he quit. He told me that he would never be as good as Segovia or John Williams, and he couldn't handle not being the best. I laughed at this. I told him that he had been great at whatever he attempted. But that wasn't enough for Rob. "The best or bust" was his motto.

Rob finally got married, and I was his best man. I had decided to never get married. Relationships seemed so complicated and messy at times, and I was a very organized person. But Rob was a faithful husband, a model parent, and raised three beautiful children. He had many careers, most of them financially unsuccessful. His wife made more money than he did. When his children grew up, they were making more money than he did. He said that this bothered him, but I didn't believe him. I think deep down, he knew that, in his father's words, he would never have to worry.

The last time I met up with Rob, we were both sixty years old. I had been retired for some time, living off my social security and doing some pickup work during tax time for extra money. Rob's father had recently died, and Rob had inherited a great fortune. He was depressed. He blamed his failures in life on the fact that he had

16

always known he would never be poor, in spite of all his efforts to the contrary. That he never "succeeded" at anything because his back was never up against the wall (I had always secretly despised his unimaginative use of clichés). Even though born with immense creativity, passion, and drive, in reality, there was no absolute need for him to fight for survival like many, if not most, of the great people, past and present. I told him to stop his whining, that he was one of the most accomplished human beings I had ever known and that he had achieved remarkable heights on many different levels. He told me that words weren't good enough—that in his own mind, he was a failure, a tortured being. I suggested that he kill himself. He laughed and told me he would but that he was a coward. A coward because he never had the guts to walk away from all his money and face life head-on, to succeed on his own merit. He told me that I was the courageous one. I laughed. But he was serious. He told me that I was courageous because I had, with very little talent, creativity, passion, or material resources, carved out a respectable life. And then added that I had succeeded in life, "In spite of yourself." I didn't laugh at this comment. After a lifelong friendship, I came to the sorry conclusion that for all his talents, Rob was an extraordinarily shallow thinker and perhaps did need some help from me to achieve his goal.

It's now my time to go. I have eaten a wonderful meal of my own choosing. Brushed my teeth. Filed my fingernails. Had my head shaved. My uniform is clean. Everything is in order. I must admit I'm a little scared, but I won't be alone. The state requires witnesses and a doctor to confirm death by lethal injection. Am I sorry that before Rob died, he suffered … No, I won't go into all the gory details. It's enough to say that I was always good at sharpening knives. And, in some ways, I think he was grateful.

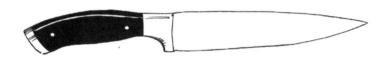

A CURIOUS NIGHT

The coast of Maine receded in the distance. The fishy salt air made John's skin itch. The rolling sea turned his stomach. He hoped he could last without having to stick his head overboard. His new girlfriend, Annie, oblivious to his suffering, or perhaps just not sympathetic—John was still getting to know her, still trying to figure out how to give her that first kiss—lounged in a deck chair, eyes closed, wisps of long blond hair swirling about.

Forty-five minutes later, a voice came over the PA system. "Rockhaven."

John, looking a wee green but relieved, cleaned his glasses with his shirttail and settled them back on his face. He and Annie watched from the main deck as the captain maneuvered the ferry into its island berth. The crew scurried about, lowering the gangplank, gathering luggage, and aiding someone in a wheelchair.

Shouldering their backpacks, John and Annie stepped onto the dock. The sensation of walking on firm ground gave him a touch of vertigo. He grabbed Annie's shoulder to regain his balance. "Sea legs," she said. "Breathe."

A voice called out from beyond the ropes. Annie grinned and ran off through the crowd. She threw her arms around a giant of a woman with short, curly red hair. Next to her stood a diminutive man wearing a frayed baseball cap. John took a deep breath and smiled. He knew Annie had been looking forward to introducing him to her old college roommate.

"John, I'd like you to meet Jenny and Angus McKenzie," Annie said, swooping her arm with great flair.

Jenny gave John a bear hug. "So, this is what all the fuss is about!"

Angus tipped his cap. "Better be gettin' on. Got quite a drive."

Jenny laughed. "Jesus, Gus, it's a ten-minute ride."

"Never know," Angus said, wrinkling his nose.

They crammed into Angus's pickup. John sat in the truck bed with the backpacks. After a pleasant drive along the coast, then inland for a half-mile or so, they turned onto a smooth dirt road, bordered on both sides by the most enticing-looking meadows John had ever seen. A small herd of grazing sheep had cropped the grass so short it looked like green velvet. He could imagine himself stroking it, lying down in it, having sweet dreams in it.

They passed an old barn. Something caught John's attention in the meadow behind it. The pickup jolted to a stop. He had to catch himself from banging his head into the rear window.

The unfinished worn clapboard of the massive farmhouse glowed like burnished copper in the setting sun. John hoisted the backpacks, jumped down from the pickup and tripped, falling right into Jenny's arms. She gave him a squeeze and let him go. "I like him, Annie. Skinny, but more meat than Angus."

Annie giggled.

Angus huffed. "Bet'cha he can't dance."

Jenny stared him down. "As I recall, you couldn't either."

A couple of hours later, bellies full of roast lamb and potatoes, a fresh garden salad, the foursome relaxed around a big wooden round table lit by candlelight. Tongues loosened by homemade wine and homegrown cannabis, the conversation was lively.

Jenny held on to one of John's arms and leaned in. "So, without even thinking, I dropped out of college and married him," she said.

"I thought she was crazy to hook up with a sheep herder who lived on an island," Annie said.

"I was!" Jenny said.

The two women burst out laughing.

John took a sip of wine. "Angus?"

Angus took a pull on his meerschaum pipe and arched an eyebrow.

"When we drove past the barn, I noticed a circle about twenty feet in diameter of what looked like mushrooms."

"Ahyut, that's what it were. A fairy ring."

"A fairy ring?" John said.

The girls stopped yakking. He noticed Jenny give a slight shake of her head to Angus.

"Doorway into the world of the little people. Don't want to go near it at night." He glanced out the window at the silver landscape. "Especially during a full moon." He handed the pipe to John, who sniffed it, made a face and passed it to Annie. She took a deep drag.

"I wasn't planning on it," John said.

Angus looked him up and down. "I wouldn't think so."

Jenny cleared her throat and clapped her hands. "Let's dance, Angus."

"Wait, why wouldn't I?" John said.

Jenny grabbed her fiddle off the wall and tuned it. "I'll tell you why. You see Angus here?"

John nodded.

"He used to be my size."

They all laughed for quite some time.

Angus had tears running down his eyes. "Big as a house. Strong as a bull."

"That's why I married him. Swept me right off my feet like I was light as a feather." She blew him a kiss.

"Now she does it to me!" Angus doubled over with laughter.

Jenny drew the bow across her fiddle.

"You two aren't making any sense," Annie said.

The bow made a squeaking sound as it stopped. "Angus here, drunk one night, wandered into the fairy ring and danced. Couldn't stop till morning."

"Lost a hundred pounds," Angus said.

"Quite some dance," Annie said.

"For someone who didn't know how," Angus said and howled with laughter.

"Thing about a fairy ring," Jenny said, "is you can't tell how it's going to work on you. Why, hear tell some people never come back."

"You never know," Angus said. "And sometimes people get bigger, and sometimes they shrink."

John laughed. "Sounds like a lot of gobbledygook to me."

"He's a math major," Annie said. "A logical fellow."

"Sounds boring," Jenny said.

John saw Annie roll her eyes. "What?"

Annie took a slug of wine. "Well, John, since we're among friends, what's the last daring thing you did?"

"Well, uh …" John stammered.

"My last boyfriend was a skydiver," Annie said, offering him the pipe.

He shook his head.

"You a ganja virgin?" Jenny said.

"Huh?" John said.

"Never smoked?" Jenny said.

"I heard it messes with your thought process," John said.

"Exactly!" Jenny said. "This is the best pot on the island. It would be insulting if you didn't give it a try."

"Skydiver," Annie said, again offering the pipe.

John took it, sucked in the burning smoke and coughed, his eyes tearing up.

Angus rose from his chair and hitched up his pants. "C'mon, John, let's dance for the girls."

"Don't know how," John said.

Angus snickered. "You're a real live wire."

Jenny rocked her bow across the fiddle strings and broke into a lively jig. Angus moved around the table, hopping on one foot, then the other. Jenny sawed away, faster and faster, until Angus was a blur of motion.

After Angus passed out on the floor in a pool of sweat, Jenny opened a door right off the dining room.

"You two can have the master bedroom tonight. We're not going to need it." She glanced back at the prone Angus and laughed.

John looked at Annie, who shrugged.

John kept his back turned as Annie got undressed and slid under the down comforter on the king-size bed. He sat down in an armchair and stared out the window.

"Cozy in here," Annie said.

"Jeez, Annie, I don't know," John said.

Annie lay back on the pillow. "This is awkward."

"I think I'm stoned," John said.

"Okay, you ponder some numbers. I'm going to sleep." She turned out the bedside light.

John stared at the moonlit flower prints on the wallpaper. Closed his eyes. Opened his eyes. Stood up, stripped down to his underwear and climbed into the bed. Annie nestled up close. She reached down between his legs, searching.

He pushed her hand away. "Don't."

She looked into John's horrified eyes. "It's okay. I get it now." She turned over and fell asleep.

John tossed and turned for a few minutes, but didn't feel sleepy. He put on his glasses and tiptoed out of the room, out of the house, and into the moonlit night. He padded across the dirt road, past the barn, and into the meadow. The dew glistened off the circle of mushrooms.

John took a deep breath and stepped into the fairy ring. He shivered and hugged himself, the night air cool against his bare skin. He studied the ground.

"Just as I thought. A bunch of mushrooms."

An owl hooted from the forest on the edge of the meadow.

He turned to leave the fairy ring when a powerful force clamped down on his brain. A sickening dizziness overwhelmed him. He fell to his knees and then onto his back. Splayed out like a snow angel, he struggled to rise but couldn't move a muscle. And then he heard something, distant at first but growing louder by the second—a terrifying buzzing sound, like a swarm of killer bees. He mouthed a soundless scream. His eyes darted. He caught a flash of movement out of the corner of his eye, but he couldn't turn his head to see what it was.

The buzzing receded, and a small bright cloud materialized high overhead. It moved towards his face. As it got closer, the buzzing increased, and he could make out tiny limbs flashing in the moon's glow. The buzzing mixed with chatter, almost human but unrecognizable as any language he was familiar with.

With a swooping motion, like a flock of starlings, the cloud descended and hovered inches from his eyes. He could see hundreds of tiny wings beating as fast as a hummingbird—and smiling little faces.

The flock disappeared. A second later, he felt a tickling sensation on his chest that worked its way down his stomach and into his groin area. The buzzing and chatter stopped. Then the chatter picked up again, with overtones of arguing. Without warning, a single fairy landed on John's glasses. He watched as she put her face to the lens and shook her head. She had sparkling blue eyes and wispy silver hair. She held her thumb and forefinger just so, making the universal sign for "small," then giggled and flew off.

The tickling sensation commenced in his groin. It grew in intensity until John felt he was about to burst, and then it stopped. Tiny cheers erupted. The flock of fairies flew past John's glasses in formation, dipped their wings, and disappeared.

John's body relaxed. He wiggled his fingers, stretched his limbs and sat up. He looked down at his lap.

"Whoohoo!" he hollered.

The owl on the edge of the forest returned his call.

The next morning at breakfast, around the old wooden table, John gobbled down a stack of pancakes. Annie was smiling.

"Well, you two look pretty happy this morning," Jenny said.

"John wandered into the fairy ring last night," Annie said.

Angus perked up. "You learn to dance?"

John looked at Annie.

She licked the syrup dribbling off his chin. "Oh, yeah."

FULL OF HIMSELF

Jason thrashed in the thick, putrid liquid. Taking in a lungful of hot, gaseous air, he disappeared under the surface, sucked down as if sinking in quicksand. His foot touched bottom. Something gripped it. Panicked, he pushed off with his free leg and came up sputtering, gagging. The wall of the cavern was only inches away from his grasp. With a violent kick, he lunged and grabbed hold of a bulge on the slimy surface. He could see a tunnel entrance at the top of the cavern.

Jason worked his way upward, one slick handhold at a time, until he reached the mouth of the tunnel. With a Herculean effort, he wedged himself up and in, his back pressing against one side, his feet on the other. He grunted and wiped slime from his face. The tunnel was pitch black, and Jason knew that once he started ascending, it would be too narrow to turn around. It was either up or fall back into the rancid lake below.

He had to dig in his heels to get even close to a firm purchase, then slide his back up as far as he could before his feet began to slip. Then start the laborious process all over again. Sweat stung his eyes. It must be a hundred degrees in here, he thought. A gust of stinking hot gas, accompanied by a loud rumble, blew up from below and engulfed him. He choked, almost losing his grip. Fresh air rushed down from above and revived him.

He couldn't tell how long he'd been inching his way up the dark chimney when he spied a dim light coming from above. His head emerged into an open space. Reaching behind, he could feel a smooth, slippery knife-like ridge. Risking it all, he thrust off from the far side with his legs and spun in mid-air like a trapeze artist. Gravity took hold, but both hands caught the ridge. He dangled from the lip and caught his breath.

He hooked one leg over the ridge and pulled himself up until he straddled it, like mounting a horse. In the faint light, he saw that he now sat between two dark holes, the one he'd just come up and another, similar in size, on the other side of the ridge. And above him, some sort of handhold hung from the ceiling, backlit with the tantalizing glow of potential freedom. He thought he heard muffled voices. I have to keep going up, he thought.

Jason raised his legs and positioned himself so that, if he was careful, he could stand up and balance as if on a tight rope. To reach the handhold, he would have to leap. Attaining an upright position, he bent his knees and then sprung up like a diver off a springboard. He missed the handhold and plummeted down the other hole as if he were on a steep waterslide.

He came to an abrupt halt and was enveloped by a spongy mass. He fought for air. The mass moved like an undulating serpent. A space opened as if he were in the jaws of some mighty beast. He crawled in the direction he had come. A gust of hot air hit him in the face and ripped him from his purchase. He tumbled deeper into the creature's maw, which closed around him in smothering darkness. I am going to die here, Jason thought. And just twenty-nine years old. I feel so good, so strong. Capable of doing anything I set my mind to. "If I just had one more chance," he yelled.

The mass expanded. A blast of air washed over Jason's body. Now, he thought. He clawed his way upward as fast as he could in the swelling, sweltering environment. He reached the entrance to the tunnel and kept moving, digging his toes into the soft sides, grabbing onto anything offering support. His hands clamped onto the ridge, and he pulled himself up in one smooth motion. He balanced for a moment on the ridge, then vaulted toward the handhold that vibrated like a ringing bell. He snagged it and held on. Swinging his legs back and forth, he built up a pendulum motion. A ferocious burst of air rushed up from beneath. Reaching the zenith of the arc, he let go and sailed on the updraft, trusting in some unknown god to deliver him from the hellhole he'd been fighting to escape.

He landed face down on a dry, leathery rock, fearing that if he moved, he would slip back down. His eyes scanned the area. A short distance in front of him appeared to be the mouth of a cave, with wide, pearly stalactites coming down from above and stalagmites rising from below. And beyond it light. Blessed light. Almost there, Jason thought. Just get past the mouth.

Outside the mouth, a middle-aged man and woman looked down on a feeble old man who lay in a hospital bed, his mouth open, lips caked with dried saliva. A doctor stood by their side.

"That will be his last breath," the doctor said, marking something on his clipboard.

The woman clutched the man's arm.

"We're doing the right thing," the man said.

"I hope so," the woman said, burying her head in the man's chest.

A nurse wiped the corners of the old man's lips with a damp cloth. Pressing up on his chin, she eased his mouth closed.

Jason had just about reached the mouth of the cave when he watched in horror as it slowly clamped shut, engulfing him in eternal darkness.

SUMMER FUN TRILOGY

I

DEAD SUCKER

The gang of six, life-long vacation playmates from the Starks and Brown clans, lounged on and around the wooden raft anchored fifty feet offshore at the head of the mountain lake. Sweetie, the Brown's nasty, snippy cocker spaniel, yapped at them as she scampered up and down the beach. Although they grew up together, at least during the summers, and their parents were the best of friends, most of the time, this group of teenagers, as is often the case, were not always nice to each other.

Pooby Starks, a freckle-faced doughy lad, lounged on the raft and watched the two Brown brothers, chubby Stinky and the younger, scrawny Princely Peter, trying to drown each other in the frigid water.

Bitsy Brown, a bucktoothed redhead, and her older sister, Slippery Sue, sat together on the raft's edge, dangling their toes in the water. They screamed and jumped back when Princely Peter surfaced at their feet and splashed them with an icy spray.

Pooby's younger sister, Red Rosie, a freckle-faced skinny thing, lay on her stomach, peering over the far edge, oblivious to all as she studied the giant sucker fish that swam a few feet below the surface. She looked with dismay at the fishing line tied to the raft that led to the hook firmly secured in the sucker's mouth.

Stinky and Princely Peter climbed up the aluminum ladder that hung off the side of the raft and plunked down on the wet, carpeted surface that smelled of dog.

"Hey, sick skin, come swim with me," Stinky called over to Red Rosie.

"Leave me alone, Stinky. I don't feel like drowning today," Rosie replied coolly, then turned to Princely Peter. "You are sick, sick, sick to torture this poor fish like this."

Princely Peter mumbled something rather lengthy under his breath.

"What was that?" Rosie asked.

"He says that a bottom feeder ain't no fish worth saving. That he's doing the lake a favor. You ever had one suck on your toe?" Stinky replied for Peter and then laughed.

Red Rosie sat up, fire in her eyes. "It's a living creature, Princely Peter. Let it go, or put it out of its misery."

Princely Peter knelt down next to Red Rosie and untied the fishing line.

"What're you going to do?" Rosie said.

Princely Peter giggled and pulled on the line until the fish dangled in the air. It twisted as desperately as a fat sucker can twist, which wasn't much, especially one worn out from trying to escape the sharp metal barb that had pierced its cold flesh several hours earlier. Peter grabbed the sucker with one hand and squeezed until its eyes bulged, almost popping out of its head.

"Stop it!" Red Rosie shouted as she jumped to her feet. "You are cruel, cruel, cruel!"

Princely Peter mumbled something.

"What?" Rosie asked.

"He asked if you wanna kiss?" Stinky answered for Peter, who thrust the sucker's head toward Rosie's face. She looked wide-eyed at the grotesque lips of the sucker, puckered up to deliver a wet slimy one on her mouth. She screamed and dove into the water. Peter cackled maniacally and dove in after her, sucker in hand.

Red Rosie swam as fast as she could toward land, Princely Peter close behind. She stumbled through the shallow water and onto the shore. Sweetie, the cocker spaniel jumped up on her and knocked her down. She scrambled to her feet just as Princely Peter made it to the beach. He held out the sucker, smooched up his lips, and made lewd kissing sounds.

"Get away from me, you murdering creep!" Red Rosie yelled and took off, running down the shoreline toward her cabin.

Peter giggled and ran after her. He swung the sucker on the fishing line until it was twirling around his head. He caught up to Rosie, and the twirling sucker slapped a slimy one on her back. She screeched and tried to run faster, but Peter was too quick. He kept spinning the sucker like a cowboy's lasso, and on each pass, the sucker's fat body managed to strike Rosie somewhere. And each time she felt the splat of the disgusting sucker on her body, she screeched like an old lady who's been caught with her bloomers down. And each time she shrieked, she could hear the other Brown kids' derisive laughter coming from the raft.

Red Rosie made it the fifty yards to the path that led up to her cabin and, with a final burst, sprinted onto the front porch. She turned and pointed her finger at the closing Princely Peter.

Gasping for breath, she shouted, "Don't you dare, or I'll get Grandma Toto after you!"

Peter screeched to a halt. The spinning sucker wound tighter and tighter around his raised arm like a tetherball around its pole. It came to a halt with a soggy thump against his skin. He turned away from Rosie's evil eye and bumped into Pooby, who ambled with his head down toward the porch.

"Hey, Pooby!" Rosie shouted at him, tears welling up in her eyes. He looked up at her sheepishly. "Thanks a lot!" She turned and tramped through the screen door. He winced when it slammed shut.

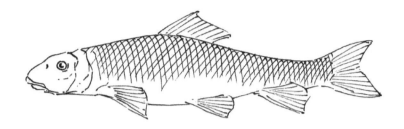

Two days later, the Starks were finishing a pleasant late breakfast. Mr. Starks was reading the paper. Grandma Toto sat in her rocker, smacking her toothless gums. Mrs. Starks sipped her coffee as she gazed out the bay window overlooking the porch and the lake beyond, from which a soft breeze floated in from the south. Red Rosie and Pooby were clearing the dishes.

"Open the porch door for me, dear," Mrs. Starks asked Pooby as she handed him her dirty dish.

He opened the door, took a quick whiff, grimaced, and then vanished into the kitchen. Sweetie, the cocker's frantic yapping could be heard coming from the Brown's yard next door.

Mr. Starks looked up from his newspaper. "Looks like we're going to have a nice day. If only that damn dog would shut up." Then went back to reading.

Mrs. Starks, coffee cup in hand, took a deep breath of the fresh air wafting in from outside. "Yes, I think you're—" Her head jerked back, and her nose wrinkled, clearly offended. Her coffee cup clattered to its saucer as she clamped a hand over her nose and mouth. "My gracious, what is that terrible smell?" she gasped.

Mr. Starks peered over his newspaper. "Now that you mention it, something is emitting a foul odor."

Red Rosie pushed open the screen door, gagged, and backed away, hand over her mouth.

"What in the world is it, dear?" Mrs. Starks asked.

Rosie made a beeline for the bathroom and slammed the door.

"Pooby!" Mr. Starks yelled. "Go see what's making that horrible stink."

Pooby came out of the kitchen and went out the screen door. Hanging from the doorknob by its fishing line was the three-day-old sucker, rotting flesh dangling from its swollen body, the rusty hook embedded in its misshapen mouth. Pooby came back in, quickly shut the main door and leaned against it.

"What is it?" Mrs. Starks asked, her hand clamped over her nose.

"Dead sucker," Pooby said.

Rosie came out of the bathroom and glared at Pooby. "Princely Peter did it."

"Those damn Brown kids," Mr. Starks mumbled from behind his newspaper.

"Put down that paper and get rid of it," Mrs. Starks ordered Mr. Starks. "Or else I'm going to get sick. And while you're at it, see if you can quiet down that horrid dog."

Mr. Starks folded his newspaper, sighed, and made to get up.

"Wait," Pooby said. He looked at Red Rosie. "Let me do it."

Once on the porch, Pooby untied the fishing line from the screen door. He glanced over at the Brown's yard, the two properties separated by the ancient eight-foot-high chain-linked fence, something the old families put there years ago to keep out the bears. To keep out the Browns, Pooby thought.

Sweetie was jumping up and down against her side of the fence, yapping incessantly. Pooby could see Princely Peter and Stinky carving on sticks outside their big teepee where, inside, he could see Bitsy and Slippery Sue setting up some kind of tea party.

Red Rosie stepped out onto the porch just in time to see Pooby approach the fence. One hand held the sucker out in front of him. The other held his nose.

Princely Peter saw Pooby coming, nudged Stinky and mumbled something. Stinky looked up and grinned wickedly at Pooby, who stopped a few feet from the fence.

"Peter wants to know if you enjoyed your breakfast," Stinky said.

Sweetie's constant yapping made it hard to understand what anyone was saying. "You say Peter stinks like a rotten sucker?" Pooby shouted.

"Sweetie, shut up! What?" Stinky shouted back.

"Here's dessert!" Pooby shouted as he flung the sucker over the fence. At that exact moment, Bitsy stepped out of the teepee, and the sucker hit her in the head. She shrieked and ran back inside the teepee.

Sweetie caught the alluring scent of rotten meat and stopped barking, her nose leading her on a zigzag course to the dead sucker that, by now, had lost more of its flesh. She dove on it and rolled and rolled, spreading putrid skin, fish guts and blood all over her body.

Slippery Sue, nose pinched closed, reached outside the teepee entrance and yanked down the canvas flap.

Stinky and Princely Peter gagged and ran off, disappearing into the bushes.

Sweetie, clearly in doggy heaven, continued to roll, desperate to spread the delicious sucker stink over her entire body.

"Here, Sweetie, time for breakfast!" Mrs. Brown called out from her cabin. Sweetie, though not finished with her job, knew a dinner bell when she heard it. She bolted for the cabin and ran in.

Pooby studied the Brown cabin as though he were awaiting the results of one of his famous science projects. Rosie, who had been watching the events unfold from her porch, stepped down and started walking towards him.

A scream exploded from the Brown cabin. A second later, Sweetie burst out the door with Mrs. Brown waving a broom in hot pursuit. Pooby and Rosie laughed as they watched Mrs. Brown chase Sweetie toward the beach.

Pooby turned to walk back to the cabin and saw Rosie standing there, beaming at him. He lowered his head and walked past her. "I did it for Mom," Pooby said under his breath and walked on.

II

SURPRISE PARTY

Slippery Sue Brown was busy setting up house in the Brown teepee, which was large, authentic, and the envy of all the other young vacationers who were lucky enough to visit nearby during the summer months. It sat in the yard, not far from the Brown's main cabin, and the Starks family next door could see it through the tall chain-linked "bear" fence that separated the two properties. It appeared as though Sue was getting ready for a tea party, placing tiny cups, saucers, and paper plates on an old checkered tablecloth draped over a makeshift table made of wood packing boxes.

Moonfaced Bitsy, the youngest of the Brown kids, ducked through the teepee's oval opening with a plate full of brownies and set them on the table. Sissy the cocker was right on her tail, charging in and making a clumsy attempt to jump up on the table and snatch a brownie. Slippery Sue caught the surprised dog by the collar and ordered it to lie down. Stinky followed, plunked down his ample rear on the ground next to the table, eyed the brownies, and said, "Let's eat!"

Princely Peter crawled in and sat down next to Stinky. He uncurled his fist and held his hand out. There, on his sweaty palm, was a small square of something partially wrapped in tinfoil that had a label on it. Stinky reached out to snatch whatever it was, but Peter clamped his hand around the tiny package.

"What do you think that is, Princely Peter?" Slippery Sue said.

Peter mumbled under his breath.

"He thinks it's chocolate," Stinky answered for Peter.

Slippery Sue laughed. "It might look like chocolate, but it's not."

Peter opened his fist and studied the object with a quizzical look.

"Well, if you're so smart, what is it then?" Stinky asked.

"Give it to me," Slippery Sue said. She held her hand toward Peter, who looked at Stinky, confused.

"I know you understand English," Stinky said to Peter.

Peter reluctantly dropped the small packet into Sue's outstretched hand. She studied it. "Just as I thought," she proclaimed.

"What did you think?" Bitsy asked.

Peter mumbled a word with a question mark at the end.

"Chocolate?" Stinky asked for him.

Slippery Sue looked around the teepee at her ignorant siblings and shook her head. "Ex-Lax," she said with a sly grin.

"What's Ex-Lax?" Bitsy asked.

"Can we eat it?" Stinky said.

"You can if you want, but I wouldn't," Slippery Sue said.

Peter mumbled something.

"He wants to know why you won't eat it," Stinky said.

"It's just for grownups. For when they can't go," Slippery replied.

"Can't go where?" Bitsy asked.

"To the bathroom," Slippery said.

"They go to the bathroom all the time," Bitsy said.

"Yes, but sometimes when they go to the bathroom, they can't go," Slippery Sue said.

"Hmm, I think I get it," Stinky said. "It's a riddle."

"You are all idiots. Just try to think for one second. What do you do when you go to the bathroom?" Slippery said.

Peter's eyes lit up. He mumbled something excitedly to Stinky.

"Brush your teeth?" Stinky translated for him.

Slippery Sue threw up her hands in frustration. "You go to the bathroom!" she yelled.

"Calm down, Slippery. We've already figured that one out," Stinky said.

Slippery Sue made a noise similar to a hungry pig grunting. "OK, let me put it another way. What do you do when you sit on the toilet?" she said, folding her arms across her chest with a professorial air.

"Read a comic!" Stinky said.

"Girls don't read on the toilet, so that's not it," Slippery replied with disdain. "Guess again."

"Go pee?" Bitsy asked.

Peter, who had been somewhat comatose during this challenging intellectual exchange, began shaking his head vigorously back and forth.

"What is it, Peter?" Stinky asked.

Peter leaned toward Stinky and mumbled vehemently into his ear. Stinky shook his head knowingly.

"He says that boys don't pee sitting on the toilet, and he's right," Stinky stated on behalf of Peter. "Now what?"

Slippery Sue surveyed her lost siblings. "I guess I'll have to spell it out for you."

Bitsy's face dropped. "I can't spell."

Slippery Sue made a sharp guttural sound and smacked herself on the head. "You poop! P ... O ... O ... P!" She glared at each one in turn as she shouted, "Poop! Poop! Poop!"

Peter's eyes widened, and he nodded up and down so fast his teeth began to chatter.

"I'm gonna tell mother!" Bitsy cried out, blushing and ashamed for her older sister.

"I'm merely describing a bodily function brought on by nature's call," Slippery Sue explained. "Ex-Lax is for grownups that can't go to the bathroom."

"Aw, we're back where we started," Stinky whined.

"Let me try one more time. It's called 'constipation.' You try to go number two but can't. So you take Ex-Lax and then watch out

41

because you're gonna go and go until there's nothing left inside you. And it hurts, too. You get cramps. I know because I heard father telling mother about it the other day."

Peter shook his head, downcast, and mumbled something.

"So now we have to throw out the chocolate," Stinky said, disheartened.

"It's not chocolate!" Slippery shouted, slamming her fist on the table and rattling the dishes. This got the other's attention. "And if you will just shut up for one second, I have a plan."

Everyone shut up.

"We're going to have a surprise party."

"How can it be a surprise if we know about it?" Stinky asked.

"Because, dimwit, it's not for any of us," Slippery Sue spit out.

"Then who can it be for?" Bitsy asked.

Slippery Sue gave them all a wry little smile. "Do you remember … the 'sucker'?

Inside the teepee, Slippery Sue, Bitsy, and Princely Peter were sitting around the little box table, trying to hold back their laughter.

Stinky fell through the opening. Sweating and out of breath, he could barely speak but managed to blurt out "They're coming!" just as Pooby and Red Rosie peeked inside.

"We always wanted to see the inside of this place," Rosie said in awe as she scanned the teepee from the dirt floor up to the smoke-hole twenty feet above her.

"You've always told us to keep out," Pooby said, always vigilant around the Browns. As he was also very smart, if not indolent and self-centered, he was a match for Slippery Sue. But she rose to the occasion.

"Come in, come in, Pooby, Red Rosie," Slippery Sue said as she made a magnanimous gesture. "Please have a seat. Dessert is about to be served. Rosie, you sit next to me."

Rosie glared at Peter, who looked down and away. He secretly liked her. That's why he liked to torture her. She went around to the other side of the tiny table and sat between Slippery and Bitsy. A dog lover, she reached out to pet Sissy, who lay close by.

"She doesn't smell so bad anymore," she said while Pooby positioned himself between Stinky and Peter.

"Let's eat!" Stinky cried out, reaching for a brownie.

Slippery Sue's hand lashed out like a striking cobra, grabbed Stinky's wrist, and flung it away from the table.

"Where are your manners, Stinky?" Slippery admonished as she picked up the brownies, arranged in a ring on the plate, and held them out in front of Pooby. "Guests first." She maneuvered the plate so Pooby would take the brownie with the Ex-Lax hidden inside.

Pooby took a brownie, but not "the one," and put it on the table in front of him. Slippery Sue frowned, then turned her attention to Red Rosie, who reached to take a brownie as Sue spun the plate to get the right brownie facing Rosie. Rosie was about to pick the wrong brownie when Slippery made a last-minute adjustment with an imperceptible turn of the plate, and Rosie's hand landed on the right brownie.

"Yes!" Sue shouted and then took a deep breath. "Go ahead and take it, Rosie. The one you're touching."

Rosie studied the brownie. She could see something shiny sticking out of it. It looked like a piece of tinfoil. She looked at Slippery Sue, who held the plate as steadily as a sniper aimed his rifle.

"What … if I don't want that one?" Red Rosie asked.

"That's the—"

"Shut up, Bitsy!" Slippery snapped at her little sister, who stuck out her tongue. Slippery turned back to Rosie. "Why, Rosie, they're all the same. So … take that one now, or perhaps you'd like to go home?"

This got Pooby's attention. "Take the brownie. We're hungry."

Rosie picked up the brownie, and Slippery Sue quickly passed the rest of the brownies around to her brothers and sister.

"Homemade brownies!" Slippery said with gusto. "Let's eat!" She chomped into her brownie and chewed. "Good and gooey," she proclaimed.

The others began eating, emitting sounds of pleasure as they swallowed the sweet treat. All eyes, except for Pooby's, were on Rosie, who faked taking a bite of her brownie but chewed convincingly. As she nodded her head with delight, her hand, hiding the brownie, slid from the table. She held it behind her back and opened it, palm up. Sweetie dove for the brownie and gobbled it up.

"Oh my!" Rosie said. "Sweetie ate my brownie!"

The Browns gasped in unison as Sweetie settled back down behind Rosie and licked her chops.

"I'm so sorry, but may I have another one?" Rosie said.

"You didn't say 'please'," Slippery Sue said with a frown.

Sweetie whined, spun her head around, and furiously licked her hind end.

"What's wrong with Sweetie?" Rosie said.

All eyes turned toward Sweetie. Peter mumbled something.

"Chocolate can kill a dog," Stinky translated.

Sweetie passed some loud gas, jumped up, and started chasing her tail. Everyone started to laugh until the smell got to them, and they collectively held their noses. Sweetie spun around violently, knocked over the table, and ran out of the teepee, tail between her legs. The gang rushed to the opening and poked their heads out just in time to see Sweetie leap onto the Browns' porch and claw at the screen door. They watched as, from inside the house, Mrs. Brown approached the screen door and put her hand on the latch.

"Don't let her in!" Slippery Sue shouted at her mother.

"Don't be ridiculous, dear. She's obviously hungry," Mrs. Brown called back as she opened the screen door, and Sweetie dove into the house.

The gang crept toward the house, curious to see what would happen next.

"Now you've done it," Slippery said to Rosie. "That's the last time we invite you into our teepee."

"I said I was sorry," Rosie said and made a sad mouth. "I didn't mean to ruin the party."

"Sweetie! What on earth do you think you're doing?!" Mrs. Brown screamed from inside the house. "You stop that this … Oh, pee-u … disgusting! What's gotten into you?!"

The screen door burst open. The children watched as Sweetie bolted out. But the poor dog wasn't fast enough to keep Mrs. Brown from smacking it on the rear end with a broom. Sweetie ran off the porch, tail between her legs, and disappeared into the nearest bush, where the gang could hear her let loose with a loud, juicy splat.

III

THE BEE STING

Before the Starks and Brown children reached puberty, their play was a lot more innocent, not as mean and vindictive as it would become during their teenage years. That being said, they still managed to get into a lot of trouble, usually instigated by one of the Brown kids, who seemed to have a nose for mischief, with their neighbors, the two Starks children, being their main target. Bitsy Brown, at six-years old, the youngest and most innocent of all, would often be the unwitting participant in her elder siblings' shenanigans.

It was a mid-July evening in the mountains. The sun had just disappeared over the ridge bordering the western shore of the lake, but at this time of year, it would be light out for several more hours, leaving plenty of time for boredom to set in and force the tender gears of pre-pubescent minds to start planning out some ridiculous prank. In this case, it was Slippery Sue Brown who came up with what her brothers, pudgy Stinky and mute Princely Peter, considered a brilliant idea—especially because it contained body parts and the possibility of getting at least one of the Starks kids in trouble.

Slippery Sue pressed her face against her side of the chain-linked fence separating the Browns from the Starks. She watched Pooby and Red Rosie Starks digging with pieces of driftwood in their stony yard.

"Hey, Red Rosie," Slippery called over, "you wanna play?"

At this point, it must be noted that although Rosie was two-years older than Slippery, which should have made her, at least during these adolescent years, the dominant female of the group, Slippery held a powerful grip on Rosie's psyche. The reasons were quite simple. Rosie was a compassionate being and would do anything for friendship. Slippery Sue was the closest one in age to being a playmate besides her brother Pooby, who, although quite brilliant, even at this young age, was also a bit removed. Besides, the Browns had, in general, more toys. The Starks were somewhat Spartan and lived a simple, though enjoyable life, whereas the Browns had the motorboats, canoes, sailfish, swim tubes, and, best of all, the teepee. So, Red Rosie was putty in Slippery Sue's hands. And Slippery had always been cunning.

Rosie stopped digging, looked up, and saw Slippery Sue leaning against the fence, beckoning her to come over.

"Me?" Rosie asked, confused, as Slippery Sue hardly ever asked her to play.

Slippery nodded vigorously. Rosie could see Bitsy playing outside the big teepee behind Slippery and was hoping that maybe, just maybe, this time, Slippery was going to invite her to play in there.

Rosie walked over to the fence. Slippery smiled at her. "You wanna play with me and Bitsy," Slippery asked nonchalantly.

"Sure," Rosie said. "Do you want to play in your teepee?" she added hopefully.

Slippery glanced around surreptitiously, then leaned in toward Rosie, who leaned in closer to her side of the fence until she could smell Slippery's breath. "No, we don't want anyone to see us. Meet us at your secret hiding place in about ten minutes," Slippery whispered conspiratorially.

"OK," Rosie said and took a step back.

"Wait!" Slippery Sue hissed. "Bring a flashlight and wear an apron. A white apron," Slippery ordered.

"What for?" Rosie asked.

"You'll find out. It'll be fun," Slippery said. "And don't tell anyone where you're going. Got it?"

Rosie nodded, and Slippery skipped over to Bitsy and said something to her. Bitsy looked up and waved to Rosie, who gave a little wave back. Stinky and Princely Peter trotted up to Slippery Sue, who cupped her hand beside her mouth and, looking over at Rosie, whispered something to them. They giggled and ran off.

Red Rosie, wearing a crisp white apron and holding a flashlight, sat on the ground in the semi-darkness, waiting for Slippery Sue and Bitsy. Years earlier, as toddlers, Rosie and Pooby had discovered this private area under the stairs leading up to Grandma Toto's house, which was situated up the small rise leading away from the Starks main cabin. Wooden slats enclosed the sides of the staircase, but on the side farthest from the footpath, a few of the slats were missing, and you could slip in or out without anybody noticing. When you were hiding there, you could peek out and spy on unsuspecting passersby, usually adults. Then, you could either be quiet until they passed, or sneak out the broken side, creep silently into the brush, and disappear.

Rosie was just about to give up on her playmates when Slippery Sue, wearing a white kerchief on her head, crawled through the narrow opening and crouched down on the ground. Bitsy crawled in after her, snagging her skirt on a splinter of wood but tearing it free without too much damage.

"I thought you forgot," Rosie said.

Slippery Sue held a finger to her lips and then whispered, "We just had to wait until we could sneak away from Stinky and Princely Peter. I hope Pooby doesn't know where you are. We don't want the boys spying on us now, do we?"

"He doesn't know, but why don't we want them to know?" Rosie asked.

"Because this is a private matter," Slippery Sue said in a low voice.

"What is?" Rosie asked.

"You don't ask the questions. I tell you what to do. Understand, Doctor Rosie?" Slippery Sue said.

"Doctor—?"

"Quiet!" Slippery hissed. "You are the doctor." She pointed to Rosie's apron. "I am the nurse." She pointed to her kerchief. "And Bitsy is the patient."

"I am?" Bitsy whispered.

"OK, sounds like fun. What's wrong with the patient, Nurse Sue," Red Rosie asked in a professional tone.

"She has a bee sting," Slippery said.

"I do?" Bitsy asked. "It doesn't hurt."

Slippery glared at Bitsy. "That's because we're playing."

"I see," Doctor Rosie said. "And where is this bee sting?"

A sly little grin spread across Slippery's face. "On her rear end."

"Oh my," Rosie exclaimed as she turned toward Bitsy. "And how did this happen, little girl?"

Bitsy shrugged her shoulders.

"She was going pee in the woods and backed into a flower with a bee in it," Slippery Sue said.

"I see," Doctor Rosie said. "Well then, I will have to examine it, won't I?"

"Yes," Slippery said. "Little girl, please get on your hands and knees."

"I don't—"

"Now, or you don't get your cookie!" Slippery whispered loudly to Bitsy, who acquiesced and got down on her hands and knees. Slippery lifted up Bitsy's skirt and flipped it onto her back.

"Now, Doctor, we will need some light," Slippery said to Red Rosie, who switched on her flashlight and shined it on Bitsy's rear end.

"I don't see redness of any kind. Where exactly is the sting?" Doctor Rosie asked.

"Head down, butt up," Slippery instructed Bitsy, who complied, exposing herself completely.

Red Rosie, embarrassed, turned away, the flashlight going with her.

"Hey, Doctor, the light, please!" Slippery said in a loud whisper.

Rosie reluctantly swung the light back around and onto Bitsy's fanny.

"I don't see any bee sting. Anywhere," Doctor Rosie said.

"It's right between the crack, and you have to fix it," Slippery Sue said.

"I don't have the right medicine. I don't have any medicine, and I have to go home now," Red Rosie said.

"And I thought you always wanted to see the inside of our teepee," Sue said with a hint of mock-sadness.

Rosie hung her head. Slippery Sue reached into her pants pocket and pulled out something.

"Give me the flashlight," Slippery said.

Rosie handed her the flashlight.

"Here's the medicine," Slippery added, handing Rosie a small red bottle.

Rosie looked curiously at the bottle, then at Slippery Sue. "This is nail polish."

"No, it's bee sting medicine, and you're going to apply it," Slippery said.

"I'm getting tired," Bitsy whined. "Can I put my butt down yet?"

"Just a minute, little girl," Slippery said, patting Bitsy on the back. "Doctor Rosie just has a small operation to perform." Then she glared at Rosie. "This is an emergency, Doctor. Get to work!"

"Oh, all right, but I don't think this—"

"Quickly! She might bleed to death!" Slippery whispered urgently.

"I don't wanna bleed to death!" Bitsy cried out.

"SHHHHH!" Slippery said. "Doctor? We're wasting time here."

Doctor Rosie unscrewed the nail polish cap, pulled out the brush, wiped it gently on the edge of the lip, aimed the brush, and slowly moved in.

"That's right, easy now," Slippery whispered with glee.

From outside the secret hiding place came a giggle. Rosie's hand stopped in mid-air. "What was that?" she asked with a timid whisper.

"Do it!" Slippery said.

Rosie's applied the paint.

"It hurts," Bitsy whimpered.

"Don't be such a baby," Slippery scolded. "You want to get all better, don't you?"

"I'm not sick," Bitsy said.

"Yes, you are. Now shut up and be a good patient." Slippery ordered, then added, "Hurry up, Doctor. The patient is getting impatient."

Doctor Rosie dipped in the polish brush and applied a few quick strokes, then returned the brush to the bottle and let out a big sigh. Bitsy collapsed on the ground and rolled into a fetal position.

"It stings! It stings!" Bitsy cried out.

Hilarious laughter erupted from outside the hiding place. Slippery turned and yelled toward the slats. "You boys better get outta here, or you'll be in big trouble!"

"It's you gonna be in big trouble. You and Red Rosie!" Stinky shouted back as he, Princely Peter, and Pooby ran off laughing into the darkness.

Bitsy roused herself into a sitting position. "My butt really hurts. I'm gonna tell mom what you did." She started to crawl out of the opening.

"But Bitsy, I didn't do anything. It was Red Rosie. Don't forget that, or you don't get a cookie," Slippery said in a patronizing voice.

Bitsy stopped crawling, looked back, and glared at Red Rosie. "You did it."

Rosie turned to Slippery Sue, incredulous. "What are you talking about? You told me what to do. I didn't want to do it."

Slippery Sue scoffed. "Well, that just goes to show how smart you are."

"Huh?" Rosie said. "I get good grades in school."

"Oh yeah? Well, everybody knows that nurses don't tell the doctor what to do," Slippery Sue said with satisfaction. She then turned to Bitsy. "Let's go get you that cookie."

BURTON & THE BULL

Burton touched his throbbing head. His hair was matted, sticky with blood. He forced his eyes to open. Thirty feet above, a faint circle of light cast dim shadows.

He moaned. It was his right leg. He could make out the vague outline of his naked body. His calf was bent beneath his torso at a sharp angle. He reached down and felt a jagged edge—his leg broken in half, splintered just below the knee. Blood oozed from the wound. He let his head fall. It hit the earth with a thump.

"Help." His voice sounded hollow, weak. Tears welled, the salt stinging his eyes. Wait. Stop. Don't panic, he thought.

He rolled onto his side, grabbed his broken leg, and enduring the excruciating pain, straightened it as best he could. Frightened and exhausted, he passed out.

Burton was jarred awake by a squeaking sound inching toward him. The circle above filled with a familiar glow.

Moon's rising, he thought.

Then it all came rushing back to him—the charging bull, his fleeing across the paddock, the ground falling away as he plunged to the bottom of the dry abandoned well.

Something hit Burton in the chest and he flung it from his body. Fearful but curious, he grabbed the object and pulled it to his face. It was a sling attached to a stout rope. He looked up and saw the silhouette of a head.

"I'm hurt," he cried out. "I have a broken leg. I'm bleeding."

"Put the sling over your head, slip it under your arms." The deep voice echoed off the cobbled walls.

"I'll try."

Burton raised himself to a sitting position, holding on to the rope to keep steady. Spreading the sling wide with his hands, he dropped it over his head and worked it around his shoulders, allowing it to drop to his waist. He tugged on the rope, relieved to feel resistance on the other end.

The full moon illuminated the shaft with a cold radiance.

Burton shivered. "I'm ready."

"Grab the rope with both hands," shouted the voice.

Burton took hold. Pulled off the ground with a jerk, he grimaced. The rope spun him in circles, his broken leg twisting.

Overcome with dizziness and pain, Burton closed his eyes. He could see himself in the cabin, leaning against the headboard of the comfortable bed, looking down at the dark-haired woman asleep at his side. Smiling at her, stroking the purple bruise on her cheek. Thinking how sorry he was. Then gazing out the window. The brilliant noon sun cast oppressive heat on the scorched earth. Across the plain, distant shapes distorted, vibrating in the shimmering heat. He could see the ranch's prize bull strutting about the secluded corral.

The woman's two-year-old son crawled under the corral's split-rail fence and waddled toward the bull's hindquarters. The child pointed at the bull and cried out with curiosity. The bull swiveled its giant head, eyed the child, and snorted. A dust cloud rose in the dry earth.

Burton jumped out of bed. Ignoring his nakedness, he bolted out the door and sprinted to the corral. He jumped the rail and ran toward the bull that now moved to face the child. Burton waved his hands wildly.

"Over here! Over here!" Burton shouted as he ran at the bull. When he got about twenty feet from the quivering animal, he veered to the left.

The bull lowered its horns. It pawed the ground with a massive hoof and then charged Burton. Out of the corner of his eye, Burton could see the child standing, arms at his sides, wide eyes frozen in confusion.

Burton ran for the far side of the enclosure. He could hear pounding hooves closing ground behind him. He reached the fence and climbed to the top rail just as the bull's horns, with the full force of its body behind it, crashed into it. Burton sailed through the air, arms, and legs flailing as if he were trying to fly. The last sound he had heard was the wail of the child.

The squeal of the pulley roused Burton. Looking up, he could see a head peering over the edge of the well. His injured leg throbbed. His heartbeat drummed in his ears. He could hear a child crying, a woman screaming.

Weakened with pain, Burton let go of the rope, his arms going limp. The weight of his body and the pull of the rope caused his arms to rise, the sling sliding up his body.

The rope tightened around Burton's chest. A hand grabbed his hair and pulled him toward the opening. He screamed. Dilated black eyes glared at him.

"You are Burton?" the man said.

Burton's mouth moved but made no sound.

The dark-haired woman's face appeared over the edge of the well, the child in her arms. "Let him go!" she screamed.

The man backhanded her. She groaned and fell out of sight. The child wailed. The man raised Burton a few inches toward the opening.

"Did you fuck my wife, Burton?" the man said.

"He saved our son," the woman cried.

"Shut up," the man said.

The man twisted his fistful of Burton's hair. Got in his face. "Did you?" His breath laced with whiskey.

Burton stared.

The man reached behind and dragged the crying child into view. "Tell me. If not, I will throw him down the well."

59

"No!" the wife yelled. She hugged the child from behind and tried to wrench him away from the man's grip.

"Tell me, Burton. Tell me now." The man inched the child and mother closer to the edge. "Do you want him to die? Do you want them both to die?"

Burton's eyes cleared. He looked at the tear-stained child, then at the woman he had left such a short time ago, remembering her warmth, her ecstasy. He looked into the burning eyes of the man and smiled.

The man released his wife and child. He pressed his lips close to Burton's ear. "Thank you for saving my son," the man hissed. And then let go of the rope.

Burton looked up to get one last glimpse of the full moon but was unable to focus.

FOOLING DEATH

Jane tapped on the bedroom door. "Time to get up, Jimmy." She waited. Put her ear to the door. "Jimmy?" She knocked more loudly. "Jimmy Johnson," she called out in a singsong voice, "if you don't come out now, you're going to be late for school." When this failed to get a response from the other side, she turned the doorknob. Locked. She gathered herself, tucked a stray lock of hair behind her ear. "One ... Two ..."

"What?" a child's faint voice answered.

Jane sighed in relief. "At least you're alive. Let's get a move on." She jiggled the doorknob. "Come on, open up." She waited, but there were no sounds of activity. "I made your favorite lunch."

"Peanut butter and jelly?" Jimmy asked, his voice closer.

"And carrot sticks."

"I don't like carrot sticks."

"Jimmy Johnson, you open that door right now, or you're going to be in big trouble."

"No."

"What?"

"I'm not coming out."

"Are you sick?"

"No."

"It's Monday. You're coming out and going to school."

"I can't."

Jane slumped down, her back up against the door. She stared across the hall at a tiny crack in the wall. "Why not, Jimmy."

"Grandpa told me not to," Jimmy said.

Jane took a deep breath. "You know we buried Grandpa yesterday."

Bob, tucking in his shirt, steamed down the hall. He glanced at his wristwatch. "Where is that boy? I'm going to be late for work."

Jane looked up at him. "He won't open the door."

"He doesn't have a choice," Bob said. "I'll give you five dollars if you come out," he hollered at the door.

After a moment of silence, "No thanks, Dad."

Bob pounded on the door. "Open that door right now, young man, or…"

Jane yanked on his trousers. "Don't act like a jerk. You'll scare him."

Bob took a step back. "You think I'm a jerk?"

"Please relax for a minute. Breathe."

Bob sat down on the floor next to Jane. "A guy at work called me a jerk the other day."

"Why?"

"Because I cut in front of him in the cafeteria line. I did say, 'Please.' Guess it didn't help that he was on crutches."

"Sounds a little jerky to me."

"I don't think he used that specific word. Anyway, I was late."

"Like today?"

Bob leaned forward. "Why won't he come out?"

"Grandpa told him not to."

Bob slapped his thigh. "I knew we shouldn't have let him see that open casket."

Jane stroked Bob's hand. "Yes, he's obviously traumatized. Let's go easy on him. At least for a few more minutes." She reached back and tapped on the door. "Jimmy?"

"What?" The closeness of Jimmy's voice on the other side of the door startled them.

"When did you talk to Grandpa?"

"On Friday when I got home from school."

Bob glared at Jane. "You let him see that babbling old codger on the day he kicked the bucket?"

"Mom was downstairs," Jimmy said.

Bob grunted. "Would you mind telling us why Grandpa told you not to come out of your room?"

"He said I would die."

"Oh my god," Bob said. "He was lying. Stop being so stubborn and come out of there right now," he said, banging on the door.

Jane put a hand on his arm. "What did you think of your father?"

"He was an as ... jerk," Bob said.

"Why?"

"Because he never listened to me. He always had to be right."

"And you want Jimmy to think of you how?"

Bob let out a big exhale. "Okay, you win."

"Jimmy?" Jane said.

"Yes, Mommy?" Jimmy answered.

"What exactly did Grandpa tell you?"

After a long pause, Jimmy finally spoke. "I'll tell if you both come in here, but you can't ever leave, so bring a lot of food and something to sleep on."

Bob jumped up. "Alright, I've had enough. Six-year-olds are required to go to school. We could be fined."

Jane got to her feet and hugged Bob. "Dear. Calm down. Something's wrong. Let's humor him. Anyway, we don't want him growing up thinking we're jerks, do you?"

Bob sighed and looked at his watch. "Let me call the office."

She gave him a peck on the cheek. "I'll get the food."

"No carrot sticks," Jimmy called out from behind the door.

Even though it was a warm and sunny spring day, Jimmy's window was closed, the shade drawn and taped to the sash so that no light could shine in. One dim table lamp gave the room an eerie glow. Two sleeping bags were rolled out on the floor. Jimmy sat on his bed, munching a donut and sipping some orange juice. Bob sat on a cooler in one corner, grumbling as he pounded his fist into a baseball glove. Jane sat on the end of the bed.

"So, tell us about Grandpa," Jane said.

"Grandpa said I better watch out."

"Okay. Watch out for what?"

"Death," Jimmy whispered.

"We're all going to die, Jimmy. Just like your goldfish," Bob piped up.

"You said he went swimming in the toilet," Jimmy said.

"Bob, let me talk to Jimmy for a minute," Jane said.

Bob picked up a softball off the floor and plunked it into his mitt. "Anyone want to play catch?"

Ignoring Bob, Jane said in her best motherly tone, "Tell me everything Grandpa said to you, Jimmy. Please?"

"He said when he was six, like me, he went to bed one night and woke up in the morning, and he was eighty and ready to die." Jimmy looked away. "And then he did."

She looked at the drawn shades. "But why do you want to stay in your dark room?"

65

"So that it's always night. It will never be tomorrow, so I won't grow old and die. I'm fooling death!" Jimmy said.

"Okay, I kind of get it. But he lived a long, long time," Jane said.

"Too long," Bob said.

"No, no, no. Grandpa said eighty years went by in one day. And then he went 'Poof!' Right in my face! I'm scared, mommy." Jimmy fell into his mother's arms and started to cry.

Jane ran her fingers through Jimmy's curly hair. "There, there. I understand. Don't worry."

"Don't worry?" Bob said, bounding off the cooler. "Grow up, son. Death is a fact of life. Don't be a chicken."

Jane gave him a dirty look. "Take a nap, Bob. As a matter of fact, let's all take a nap." She curled up with Jimmy and closed her eyes.

Bob plunked down on a sleeping bag and, with a ball and mitt on his chest, stared at the ceiling. Within a few minutes, he was snoring.

Jane looked at Jimmy. His eyes were closed, his breathing steady. She eased away from him and snuck out of the room.

Jimmy, snuggled in his sleeping mother's arms, opened his eyes, yawned, and grabbed a bag of chips. The rattling bag woke up Bob, who sat up and looked at his watch. "Do you know what time it is?"

Jimmy threw the bag in the air. "La, la, la, la, la," he sang out, covering his ears with his hands. "Don't tell me! Take it off! Hide it!"

Jane woke with a start. "What's happening?"

"He doesn't want to know what time it is," Bob said.

Jane sat up. "Of course, he doesn't."

"It might be tomorrow!" Jimmy said.

"Put the watch away," Jane said.

"I'm going to tell what time it is!" Bob said. He stood up, took off his watch, and dangled it in front of him as he walked toward them.

Jimmy buried his face in a pillow, hands still over his ears.

Jane put her hand out, a signal to stop. "Bob, it's time for *you* to grow up," she said quietly. She motioned to him. "Come, sit on the bed with us." He did. She arranged herself cross-legged, then reached under the comforter, brought out a big book, and placed it on her lap.

"Where did that come from?" Bob asked.

"A little fairy brought it while we were sleeping," Jane said.

Jimmy yanked his head away from the pillow. "A fairy was here? What is it, Mom?"

She smiled. "A picture album."

Jimmy crawled over and got close. "Can I see?"

"Sure," Jane said. She opened the album.

"A cowboy!" Jimmy said.

"That's Grandpa when he was in his twenties," Jane said.

"He did love to ride," Bob said.

"He looks cool," Jimmy said.

They flipped through the pages, each one a picture of Grandpa doing something exciting, either by himself or with young Bob.

Jimmy pointed. "Who's that with the fish?"

"That's your father," Jane said. "And the man standing next to him is Grandpa."

Jimmy looked at Bob. "I want to go fishing."

"I'd like to take you," Bob said.

Jane turned the page.

Jimmy looked closely at the picture of Grandpa bouncing a baby on his knee. "Who's that?"

Jane smiled. "That's you when you were six months old. Grandpa loved you so much, even when you were a poopy baby."

"Mom!" Jimmy called out.

Bob continued to page through the album.

"Dad?" Jimmy said.

"Yes?"

"I don't think Grandpa was a jerk."

Bob ruffled Jimmy's hair. "I shouldn't have said that. I'm sorry." He went over and sat on the cooler. He picked up the mitt and ball.

"Hey, Dad. Throw it," Jimmy said.

Bob tossed the ball. It hit the lamp, which crashed to the floor. The room went dark.

"Uh oh," Jimmy said. "How are we going to find the food?"

"I'm sitting on it," Bob said. "Keeping it warm."

"Very funny, dear," Jane said.

"Now what?" Bob asked.

"It's okay. We're all going to live forever," Jimmy said cheerfully.

"In the dark," Bob said.

They fell quiet for what seemed a long, long time.

A loud *thunk* on the windowpane broke the silence.

"What was that?" Bob said, feeling his way to the window. "I'm going to open the shade."

"Wait! Don't!" Jimmy cried out. "It's Billy. He throws up a piece of dirt when he wants me to come out and play."

"And you don't want to go?" Jane asked.

"Well, I kind of do, but ..."

69

"Grandpa played a lot when he was a boy," Bob said. "He used to tell me about all his adventures. And a lot of them were outside," he added. "Playing with his friends."

The room fell silent ...

"You know what?" Jimmy said.

"What?" Jane and Bob answered in unison.

"I think I want to go out and play," Jimmy said. "I might as well have fun before I die." He slid off the bed and ripped the tape from the shade. He smiled and waved when he saw Billy below. "I'll be right down!" he yelled, then turned to his mother and father. "But I want you guys to stay in here so that you live a long, long time."

REFLECTION IN A MOTEL MIRROR

Harold Brown was sound asleep in a motel bed. In the buff, as usual. Before he married, he always slept in pajamas, but his young wife insisted he sleep in the nude. She loved the feel of the four-hundred-count cotton sheets on her bare skin, a luxury they couldn't afford, but he wanted to make her happy. And Harold got to like it, too. Besides, nestling up to a warm body on a cold winter morning was almost as good as the first cup of coffee.

He was on his way to Des Moines to visit his daughter Susan and two grandchildren. She had recently gone through a messy divorce with an abusive husband. Harold had been having nightmares about her, his baby and youngest of three, ever since she had called to tell him about a broken nose and restraining order.

Harold was a widower and retired, so he had the time for a trip. He'd been on the road for two days, starting off in Rhode Island. Driving solo cross-country, something he hadn't done since his twenties, had brought back fond memories. He had even found himself smiling at his reflection in the rear-view mirror. He had called Susan after settling into his room and told her that he was somewhere in Illinois and would probably make it by early evening the next day.

He dreamed about playing on his high school football team, but this time as a full-grown man, and how invincible he felt as he knocked down one kid after another. He felt ecstatic when he woke up to relieve himself. He got out of bed and, still in a semi-dream state, was disoriented—he didn't know where he was. Then it came to him that he was in a motel room, but he still couldn't remember where the bathroom was. He stood there for a moment to let his eyes adjust to the dim glow of dawn coming through a crack in the curtain. He spied the vague outline of a door and, unsure of what lay in his path, eased himself toward it.

He could see a faint glint of light off the chrome doorknob and reached for it. At that very instant, a hand reached out from the other side to meet his. He looked up and saw a dark, terrifying human form with wrinkled skin and a grotesque head coming toward him. He recoiled in horror, then felt a crushing pain in his chest and crumbled to the floor.

When he didn't show up the next night, Susan called the motel. The woman on duty said that there was no answer in his room, and Susan asked her if she would check on him, joking that he was old and maybe forgot where he was going. The woman laughed. "Been there," she said. "Call you back in a minute."

By the time the ambulance arrived, there were several onlookers and the woman on duty all peering into Harold's room. He was sprawled naked and dead on the floor in front of the full-length mirror that hung on the outside of the bathroom door. A puddle of urine beneath him—a Rorschach inkblot on the industrial carpet.

TINY TEARS

Norman Blackheart was sad and had been from the start. Slipping from the womb into the world, he didn't cry as most babies do. He whimpered, tiny tears seeping down his little chubby cheeks in a steady stream. There was nothing his poor mother Norma could do to appease him, and she tried every trick in a mother's book—breastfeeding, warm baths, rubbing the soles of his feet, long peaceful walks in the woods, swaddling him in soft cotton, and singing lullabies as she rocked him in the old rocker on the front porch. Day after day, he wept soft, quiet tears.

His father, John, was a rugged man, a logger. "How can I? He acts like a little girl," was his usual response to Norma's plea to "Just treat him like a normal boy." And before storming out the door to take solace in the outhouse, he'd add, "And he, or whatever it is, never shuts up." The night of Norman's fifth birthday, John walked out and never came back.

"Maybe it's because you gave him a woman's name," said Gert, Norma's closest friend in her sewing circle.

"Jeez, Gert, it's not a woman's name. Sure, it sounds like Norma, but it's Nor-man. Man. He's a man. Well, not yet, but he's definitely a boy. You've seen it," Norma said.

He was still a suckling infant when Norma and John called in the village seer, an old crone with beady eyes who predicted the future for all newborns. She tickled Norman's ribs and feet, got up in his baby face, and went, "Goo-goo-gaga." Norman blinked, and tears fell from his big blue eyes. The seer recoiled.

"Ha! Ain't got no funny bone," she said. "I'd drown him."

But Norma persisted, even after John left. She put up with the gossip, even the neighborhood children's ridicule, and cared for Norman as though he were a typical child, even though, along with his constant tears, he had never spoken a word. She did laundry and ironing to make ends meet, and even taught little Norman how to balance on the footstool and hang the wash out to dry, showing him first how not to soil the clean linens. Being a boy, his face was often dirty, and when the tears ran down his cheeks, he'd swipe at them with his hands, then put those grimy mitts to the bleached whites. She showed him how to use his sleeves to wipe his face. And to not forget his nose, stimulated by the tears, that was always runny. He was quick to catch on to the rest, and it wasn't long before he was stirring laundry in the big tub. Putting it through the wringer was when he seemed to come the closest to looking happy. It was a great effort to turn the big handle with his small arms. Before each crank, he'd take a deep breath through his nose, cheeks expanding, mouth widening, and Norma could swear he was smiling.

Gert observed this behavior on one occasion and said, "Ain't a smile. My old man looks the same when he's about to belch."

The final step in his laundry education was learning how to iron. He was eager to do it, but Norma held the hunk of forged metal, hot off the wood stove, just out of reach of his grasping fingers, pleading with him to speak.

"Just one word, Norman," she said. "It's easy: Eye-run. Can you try that?"

Norman scrunched up his nose, clamped his eyes shut, and squeezed out some tears.

Norma held the iron a little closer to his outstretched hands. "Eye ... Run. Say it, Norman. Say it. For your momma."

Norman collapsed to the old plank floor, writhed on his back, kicked his feet, and screamed bloody murder. Tears fell like rain. Norma placed the iron in his little hands and smoothed back his hair.

"There, there, little Normy," she said. "Momma teach you how to iron."

Norma was secretly relieved when she sent Norman off to first grade. It was never certain if he ever slept because of the constant sniveling—though he did have enough energy during the day to keep shedding tears—so her nights were fitful, and now she would finally be able to get a few hours of sleep. But the schoolmarm sent him home for good after two days.

"I got fourteen of them in one room, and no one pays attention, to begin with," she said to Norma. "And with Norman always weeping, the other children tease him unmercifully, and, frankly, it's driving me crazy. I don't know how you stand it."

Shunned by his classmates, Norman withdrew even further into himself. Whimpering, tears dripping, he took up in the old rocker on the front porch and rocked. Night and day. Through all seasons. Norma would throw a blanket over him during the winters, which, thankfully, were fairly mild in their parts. And between doing double loads and triple shifts of laundry—he wasn't helping anymore—she'd bring him his breakfast, lunch, and dinner.

"Feed him and keep him warm. Least a mother can do," she told Gert, who wondered what the hell Norma was doing, letting her life slip away by working herself to the bone for her no-count son.

The years passed. Norman grew into a middle-aged man with long greasy hair and a shaggy beard, doing nothing with his life but rocking on the front porch. Before he had abandoned his family, Norman's father, John, had done one thing worthy of a good parent, even if it was out of desperation to try and shut up his strange and somehow terrifying offspring—on occasion, he had read comic books to Norman, whose favorite was 'Samson and Delilah'. Little Norman bawled when Samson pushed down the temple pillars and was crushed under a pile of stone rubble. After hearing that story, he never allowed Norma to come close to him with a comb or pair of scissors.

Norma grew more fragile with age and finally had to tell Norman that she was so sorry that they were running out of food and only had enough money to last a few more days. That she was sick and too weak to work any longer and was going to die soon. Norman brushed the oily hair out of his eyes, took her hand, looked into her eyes, and cried.

A short time later, Norma passed away. This was a trying time for Norman. After all the years of eating, sleeping, and drinking moonshine in the rocker, he was not in good physical condition. Yes, his calf muscles were toned from pushing off of the porch deck to keep the rocker going, but he had a huge belly that challenged his balance whenever he got up, which had only been to relieve himself in the outhouse. The only way he knew that Norma was no longer with him was when he got thirsty, and she didn't respond to his foot-stomping, the only means of communication they had developed over the years. One stomp for food, two for milk, water, or juice, and three for moonshine, which he had developed a taste for quite by accident when he discovered one of John's forgotten bottles tucked away in the outhouse rafters. Norman found a shot complemented his tears—the more he drank, the more he cried, the more he cried, the more he drank.

From that day forward, he demanded, by waving the empty moonshine bottle in Norma's face while stomping in threes, that she had better keep him supplied. It was the only time that Norma looked scared in Norman's presence and, not wanting to offend her dear, sweet, and only child, thought it best to keep a couple of bottles in the house at all times. Acquiring moonshine was an expensive and, at the time, an illegal and dangerous endeavor, but a mother's instinct for keeping her child happy outweighed the consequences.

Norma hadn't had any close contact with the community since John had left her. He was the partygoer, she the dutiful wife. She never went anywhere without him and, since the birth of Norman, had hardly left the house. Now she was a spurned spouse and shunned by her once closely-knit sewing circle. There was one place she did go, and that was to the Sunday service at the non-denominational Poor Lost Sheep Church, Pastor Lawrence (call me "Larry") Bean presiding. The men folk got a kick out of calling him "String" or "Lean," but the women called him Larry and couldn't help but giggle when he'd wink at them. Norma would sneak in late for the service and sit in the back so as not to be noticed, then leave just before it ended so that she wouldn't have to endure the whispers and sidelong glances of her former friends.

Pastor Bean fancied himself a ladies' man and, figuring that women were suckers for men in uniform, and he sure as hell wasn't cut out to join up and risk being maimed or killed, went to great lengths to present himself as a true man of the cloth, with accompanying cleaned and crisply pressed white robe, scarlet vestment trimmed in gold, a dab of rouge on his otherwise pale and pockmarked cheeks, and straight black hair (which he thought was his strongest feature) slicked back in a pompadour with a thick layer of Dr. Solomon's Pomade.

Being a church with a pastor of dubious origins, there was no call, let alone qualification, for hearing confession. But it was common knowledge passed on by the sewing circle that if Pastor Bean was slipped a request in note form and perhaps a silver dollar or two, he would be happy to meet in the vestry after hours. After offering a glass of moonshine—he received an ample supply from his more guilt-ridden male parishioners—to his "women only" customers, he'd hold their hands and smile serenely as sins were confessed. Give them a kiss on both cheeks and a 'Bless you, my child' when they parted.

His ministering to the ladies was the perfect excuse for the men to stop coming to church altogether. Neither their wives nor Pastor Bean missed them, but the offerings fell off because of it, and the church's coffers dwindled. Bean had stockpiled some moonshine— which he had developed a liking for, perhaps even a dependency on—but it wouldn't last for long.

Norma was Pastor Bean's laundress and took great pains to make sure that he looked the part. Once a week, he would bring her a load of dirty vestments. Passing by Norman rocking on the porch, he would give him the sign of the cross and a "Bless you, my son".

Norman would weep, of course. Near Norma's end, Bean was her only customer, and she had to choose between being paid in cash to buy food or in moonshine to quench Norman's endless thirst. Norman's relentless three stomps made the decision for her.

But with Norma now gone, Norman was desperate. Having no food was one thing, but without moonshine to feed his tears, for the first time in his life, they had dried up. Weakened by lack of nourishment, he was crawling on his knees towards town, empty moonshine bottle sticking out of the back pocket of his overalls, his vision impaired by his long, tangled hair, when Pastor Bean, who couldn't see where he was going for the giant pile of dirty clothes he was carrying, fell on top of him. They wrestled on the dirt road until the dust cleared, and they both recognized each other.

Pastor Bean spit gravel. "Just the man I'm looking for."

Norman glared and stomped his foot three times, raising more dust.

Pastor Bean gave him a quizzical look. "Where are your tears?"

Norman yanked the empty bottle from his overalls and waved it in Bean's face, clipping the pastor's nose and making it bleed.

"Ow." Bean rubbed his nose, spreading blood on his rouge-less cheeks. "You want moonshine?"

Norman bobbed his head up and down until his teeth rattled.

"Will that make you cry?"

Norman smiled for the first time in his life.

Pastor Bean looked at the heap of now dirtier clothes strewn about the road. "Did your momma teach you how to wash clothes?"

Norman nodded.

"Iron?"

Norman nodded.

Pastor Bean's eyes lit up. "I think I just had my first eureka. Maybe I truly am an enlightened man of the cloth."

Sunday morning at ten o'clock sharp, Pastor Bean stood at the pulpit, immaculately dressed and smartly pressed. Behind him, a ten-foot-high red velvet curtain stretched from wall to wall. He was beaming from ear to ear, his cheeks more red than usual after an extra shot of moonshine in preparation for his sermon. He gazed out over his meager flock of lost sheep and cleared his throat.

"Verily, I say unto you, behold the miracle that has blessed our humble abode of the faithful." Pastor Bean clapped his hands, and two freshly scrubbed altar boys pulled the curtain aside.

A gasp from the faithful made Pastor Bean's ears pop. A murmur swelled up and down the pews.

Norman, with a beatific smile, draped in royal blue with hair and beard neatly trimmed, sat in his rocker and rocked. And wept.

Pastor Bean raised his arms, his eyes fixed on the heavens, and said, "I bring to thee Saint Norman, patron saint of sorrow. Weep, my children, weep."

The congregation wept. Norman pulled a flask from under his robe and drained it. He scowled at Pastor Bean, who clapped his hands three times. To his flock, this signified the Holy Trinity, a religious concept he was still trying to grasp. He preached on it regularly, figuring repetition promoted understanding, but to the altar boys it was the code (prearranged with Norman) for more

80

moonshine. One of them slipped Norman a fresh flask, and his saintly smile returned.

"There, there, children," Pastor Bean said with a kind, fatherly voice. The flock, verily wailing by now, hushed, sniveled, blew noses, and patted dry their damp eyes. "To feel sorrow is to suffer," he continued. "To suffer is to feel compassion ... to feel compassion ... is to love."

A collective "Amen!" rattled the stained-glass windows.

Pastor Bean raised his eyebrows. "Faithful ones. We are in dire straits. This shelter of hope is in grave danger of being repossessed by the devil. Our flock is dwindling, donations are down, and the bottom line is that we lack the funds to pay our bills. "We ... Need ... More ... Sheep!"

A cheer went up from the congregation.

Warming up to his newfound awakening, Pastor Bean puffed out his chest. "You must go forth into the world and spread word of our miracle."

He glanced over at Norman, who was motionless and snoring. He gave him a swift kick in the shin. Norman's eyes sprung open, and he farted, setting the rocker in motion. Tears fell from his eyes.

"As I was saying," Pastor Bean said, "you must spread the gospel of the one who sheds endless tears for the suffering of mankind—our own Saint Norman of the Perpetual Tears!" Furrowing his brow and pointing toward the entrance, shouted, "Now, go ye forth!"

Inspired by their inflamed pastor, the faithful scrambled for the exit.

"Wait! Hold ye back, mighty flock!"

The faithful halted in their tracks and turned toward the pulpit.

Pastor Bean smiled sweetly. "Lest I forget, there's one more thing. Through a complex method of communication with Saint Norman, a mute, uneducated, spiritual savant, he has informed me that we are now an official church and will be offering, along with our popular confessional (a twitter rose from the faithful), a blessed communion."

Some of the faithful swooned and fell to their knees. Others babbled and spoke in tongues. Pastor Bean held up his hand. The hall quieted.

"And, as I understand, the sacrament is normally wafers and wine, but in our case, which we must all agree is very special—"

"Praise Saint Norman!" shouted a parishioner. Others took up the chant. "Praise Saint Norman! Praise Saint Norman!"

Pastor Bean pounded on the pulpit. "Enough!"

A hush fell over the faithful.

"In our case, as I have been informed by our saint, we're not talking about blood, but tears, and tears not being red, but a crystal-clear liquid, symbolizing purity and light, along with the wafers we will be serving ... moonshine!"

The faithful looked befuddled.

"So, now, go ye forth unto the masses and return thee with new converts. If you can't find any, no worries, but don't bother coming back unless you bring plenty of white lightning!"

NATURE TAKES ITS COURSE

I was eating dinner alone for the first time in months. My wife had gone to Boston to visit our daughter and grandchild for the weekend, and I was looking forward to some downtime. Maybe a little work in the garden, write some overdue letters. I had no plans, and it felt great. Then the phone rang.

"Hello?"

"Hi, Jack."

I knew the voice well. "Hi, Sylvia, how're you doing?"

"You know, maintaining ... waiting."

I fumbled with the phone.

"Jack?" she said.

"Yes?"

"Could you come over tomorrow morning and sit with Robert? Our hospice volunteer canceled, and I need to do some shopping."

Robert, my closest friend since childhood, had been fighting cancer for six years. I'd last seen him five weeks ago when he'd insisted that we go on a hike. Even with the help of his lion-headed cane, he could only shuffle along. But, in spite of his jaundice and distended belly, he didn't look too bad. He was full of life—what little was left of it.

"Jack?"

"Sorry, Sylvia. Nan's gone, and I was just thinking about all the chores she wants me to do."

There was silence at the other end.

I wasn't good with death. I think it started when I was eight and saw my grandfather in his coffin. The rouge on the cheeks of his waxen face made him look like a clown from hell. I'd even turned down my brother years ago when he called to tell me that if I wanted to see mother, I'd better come right away. That she only had days to live.

"Sylvia?"

"I understand, Jack." Sylvia's voice sounded so small. "Thanks anyway."

Shit, I thought. My best friend. "Wait."

"It's okay. I can call someone else."

The phone felt clammy in my hand. "I'll do it."

"You sure?"

"No."

We both laughed.

I pulled into their dirt driveway the next morning in my trusty pickup. I sat and looked at the old cape, marveling at how these two sophisticated people lived so simply. Sylvia came out and, after a hug, handed me a list that we went over.

"Diapers?" I said. "I don't think..."

She patted my arm. "He's not eating much, so it's no big deal. Literally."

"Right, good one. How do I know when?"

"The smell."

"Of course. That's it, then?"

"He's been acting a little weird."

"You mean normal?" I laughed.

Sylvia frowned. "Last week, I found him on the floor. Asked him what he thought he was doing. He said voices were calling him."

"Weird."

"He was going to jump out the window. To meet the voices."

I shook my head. "On second thought, maybe I'm not the man for the job."

"Don't worry. I moved him to the guest room downstairs. Besides, he's so weak he can't even lift his head." Her lips tightened, and she glanced away for an instant. I could see that she was holding back tears. "He wants to die, Jack."

"He is dying."

"Now. He says he's bored."

I laughed. "He's never been bored a day in his life."

"With the whole process," she said.

I waited.

"He says that dying is boring. Wants to get it over with."

I moved to take her hand, but she withdrew.

"And he's angry with me because I won't help him," she said, then got in her car and drove off.

Robert was asleep when I sat down on the edge of his bed. I had a hard time looking at him. The few remaining strands of hair dangled wildly from his head. His face bothered me the most. Yellow, taut skin, which looked more like parchment, compressed his once aristocratic features into a macabre mask.

I gazed out the open window at the passing clouds. As a child, I had always been able to imagine something taking shape in them, like a whale or even a rabbit. I even had vivid memories of a pirate ship. But today, there was nothing. Just clouds.

Robert moaned. I turned and watched, transfixed, as his boney fingers grasped for some unseen object. I touched his hand. His eyelids fluttered open. There was confusion in the rheumy blue eyes, but they cleared with recognition. He said something I couldn't make out. I bent down closer to his mouth.

"Help," Robert said, his breath foul.

I backed off. "Anything." I had Sylvia's list on what baby food to serve, the value of ice chips, and even how to change diapers. I winced at that thought. She'd told me not to worry about making a mess, however bad. That she was used to cleaning up.

"Closet."

"Closet?"

Robert gave a slight nod and then closed his eyes.

I opened the closet's louvered door and was hit with the scent of leather and oil. Hunting jackets and caps hung on hooks. Worn boots lined the floor. An array of shotguns and rifles leaned against

86

the walls. Robert was a Renaissance man—artist, musician, poet, linguist, and historian, but, before all else, a hunter. Since we had been boys, one of our greatest pleasures had been stalking wild birds and small game in the Green Mountains surrounding Robert's home. We spent hours in silent camaraderie, interrupted by the occasional sudden flush of grouse and report of a shotgun blast.

I glanced back at Robert. I had a good idea of what he was asking. We'd even joked about it when we were young, the different ways to end our lives if we were badly wounded or terminally ill. My favorite idea had been to jump out of a plane without a parachute. Robert's was to be eaten by a shark. We had agreed to help each other if we could, a childhood pact signed in blood around a campfire.

I closed the closet door. "Nothing in there."

"No shark," Robert said.

I smiled. "Definitely no sharks."

Robert tensed. "No shark."

"Well, if you think I'm going to eat you, you're mistaken. I'm a vegetarian now." I laughed.

"Deer," he hissed. "Remember?"

I sighed, never forgetting the wounded deer we had come across while hunting as teenagers. Panic in its eyes, it thrashed on the ground, struggling to rise. One of its hind legs flopped grotesquely, the ends of shattered bone sticking out through shredded skin. What should we do? Robert had asked. Let nature take its course, I had said, sickened by the sight of blood and impending death. Okay, Robert had said, walking up to the deer and shooting it in the head.

Jesus, I thought, staring at Robert. I had to stall for time, hoping that Sylvia would get back before things got too crazy. I went to the closet and grabbed the Smith & Wesson .38 snub-nosed revolver off a shelf. Checked it for ammunition.

I sat back down on the edge of the bed, revolver in hand. "What do you want me to do? Shoot you?" I forced a laugh.

Robert's lips tightened. He raised his arm but grimaced and let it drop. His lips moved.

I leaned in. "What?"

"Hand," Robert spit out.

I figured he was too weak to do any damage and placed the pistol in his hand. He closed his fingers around the grip and made a futile effort to lift the gun.

"Mouth," he whispered.

"What?"

"In mouth."

I looked at my watch and stood up. "I gotta go."

I stood in the kitchen, not sure what to do next. I saw Sylvia's list on the counter, read it, then crumpled it up and threw it across the room. I sat down at the table and buried my head in my hands. I remembered the last time I had seen my mother, how she waved goodbye as I boarded the plane, a tender smile on her face. I had known then that I wouldn't be able to face her again when the time came, but at least this last image was a happy one.

A gunshot exploded down the hall. I bolted from my chair, tipping it over, and ran to Robert's room, bursting through the door. He gave me a sheepish grin. I picked the gun up off the floor. There was a bullet hole in the splintered baseboard.

"Alright, you old son of a bitch, if this is what you want."

I put the gun in Robert's hand and wrapped his fingers around the grip. Helped him slip the barrel into his mouth and cringed as he tried to squeeze the trigger. The barrel slid out. Robert looked crestfallen.

"Jack?"

I shook my head no.

"Coward." The word delivered with clarity and venom.

I stumbled backward. Robert glared at me. I looked out the window, the sky a clear blue. I felt like throwing up and sucked in some fresh air. Then I laughed until I doubled up and collapsed onto the floor. I crawled to the bed and pulled myself up.

"You're goddamn right," I said, laughing.

I slid the gun barrel into Robert's mouth and wrapped my fingers around his. Robert's eyes lit up. I tightened my grip. That's when I heard a car pull into the driveway.

I splashed cold water on my face at the kitchen sink. Sylvia walked through the door and plunked down a grocery bag on the table.

"I know I'm back early. How'd it go?"

"How did it go?" I wiped my face with a dishtowel. "Interesting." I laughed. "He's as ornery as ever. It was good connecting with him, though. He always seems to teach me something."

"Thanks, Jack. I just needed some time."

"No problem. But you were right."

"About what?"

"The dying thing. He asked me to shoot him."

Sylvia laughed. "Did you?"

I smiled. "No." Gave her a peck on the cheek and opened the front door. "I also didn't change his diapers."

"Coward," she said.

MAN OF HABIT

Charlie turns the lever from hot to cold and grits his teeth. Water cascades over his naked body until he shivers. He shuts down the shower and grabs a towel.

He sits on the edge of his bed and pulls on a sock. Shakes his head 'no', takes off the sock. Studies it.

His wife, Bea, in bed, watches him. "What are you doing?"

"Wrong damn sock."

She laughs. "Sock's a sock, Charlie."

"That's true when they're fresh, but once you've worn them, they contour to that particular foot, and if you put them on the wrong one, as I've just done, it doesn't feel right." He puts the sock on the other foot. "That's better."

Bea cocks her head. "You're serious."

He smiles at her. "Dear, order is at the root of all success, as I've told you many times."

Bea gazes out the window. "Many times."

Downstairs, Bea steeps her tea at the kitchen counter and watches as Charlie pours a small amount of coffee out of his cup into the sink. He looks into the cup and nods.

"Just right," he says.

"Just right for what?" she asks.

"For the right amount of cream. If there's not enough, the mix is off and I don't enjoy it."

"I've always wondered why you did that. Every morning."

"Just a habit."

"You're a creature of habit."

"Not really. I just like doing certain things the same way." He pours some cream into his coffee.

She rolls her eyes. "A lot of things."

He pats her hand. "You know me, dear. Mr. Consistency. Now, if you don't mind, I've got to make my lunch."

"Let me guess. Peanut butter and jelly."

Charlie drives to work. He gets out of his car and presses the remote key to lock it. The headlights flash. He presses the remote again. He smiles when the car honks.

At noon sharp, he eats his sandwich, licking the edges to keep the oozing peanut butter and jelly from dripping.

He comes home from work after dark. He locks his car once, then twice. It honks.

He stands in the vestibule and turns off the outside porch light. He hangs up his coat and hat and checks to ensure he's turned off the light.

He walks into the living room, where Bea sits watching the evening news. He holds out his clenched fist.

"Guess," he says.

Bea sighs. "Just give it to me."

The next morning, after his hot and cold shower, Charlie struggles to find the right sock for the right foot. Bea lies in bed, staring at the ceiling.

"You know that little chocolate kiss you bring me every night after work?" she says.

He grins. "My favorite time of day."

"After four years, it's getting boring."

Charlie drops a sock and swivels his head. "But I thought—"

"There's a man at my office who puts a special treat on my desk—a different one every day. He's quite handsome."

"What? Are you having an affair?" He picks up the dropped sock.

"I'm just trying to point out that maybe Mr. Consistency is such a creature of habit that you can't do anything except the same thing, over and over, day after day."

He puts the right sock on the right foot. "Using the word 'creature' implies a lower level of evolution. I could get offended."

Bea throws up her hands. "Okay, Charlie, how about 'man of habit'?

He nods. "That's better."

After finishing their breakfast, Bea loads her dish and bowl into the dishwasher. Charlie lowers his dish towards the rack and freezes. He picks out Bea's dish and places it in a different spot.

"Bea," he says over his shoulder. "Remember, dishes in one row, bowls in another."

Bea screams.

Charlie spins around, dropping his bowl. It hits the floor and shatters. Bea pulls on her hair. He wraps her in his arms. "What's wrong, dear?"

She pushes him away. "What do you think?"

He gives her a sheepish grin. "I'm a man of habit?"

She grabs one of his hands. "Charlie, can you please try to change? Just a little?"

"Why?"

"Isn't it dull doing the same things the same way all the time?"

"It's practical. I don't have to think much."

She snorts. "That's obvious."

He takes his hand away. "Let's not get nasty. I think a lot. It's just that it frees me to think about more important things."

"Like what?" she says.

He looks at the shards of bowl scattered at his feet.

"Stumped, huh?" Bea says. "What about how to load the dishwasher in the proper order?"

He slumps down in a chair. "Okay, I think I get it. I'm going to vow to spend the day without doing the same old thing. Just for you."

Bea gives him a big kiss. "Oh, Charlie, that would make me so happy."

He looks into her eyes. "Starting tomorrow."

The next morning in the shower, Charlie remembers his promise to Bea and turns the lever off, but his hand stops at cold. He grabs his wrist with his other hand and tries to force the lever to move, but his hand on the lever is too strong. After a minute under the icy flow, his skin turning blue, he's able to turn it off.

He sits on the edge of his bed and studies the contours of a sock. He tries to put it on the wrong foot but can't get past the toes. He throws down the sock in disgust and slides his bare feet into his shoes.

Finished with breakfast, Bea watches Charlie's trembling hand try to place his bowl in the dish row. It's just about there, but with a spasmodic jerk, it ends up in line with the other dishes.

"Interesting," Bea says under her breath, then, "I made you lunch," and hands him a paper bag.

Charlie peeks in. "I've never eaten a tuna sandwich."

"There's a whole other world out there, Charlie."

Throughout the day, Charlie makes every effort to change his ways, but each attempt fails. Trying to eat Bea's sandwich just about brings him to tears—there are no oozing jelly edges to lick.

Arriving home after work, he can't stop himself from double-checking the porch light.

He trudges into the living room and approaches Bea, his clenched fist held toward her.

"Don't do it, Charlie," Bea says.

Charlie inches closer.

Bea puts her hands behind her back. "Try, Charlie."

Charlie grimaces. A bead of sweat trickles off his nose. He opens his hand and drops the chocolate kiss in her lap.

Bea picks it up between thumb and forefinger, like it's a dirty diaper, and plunks it in a bowl along with hundreds of others.

Charlie collapses into his easy chair and buries his head in his hands. "Oh, Bea, I'm so sorry. I feel like I've been taken over by aliens. I have no control. How did I get this way? What am I going to do? I don't want to lose you. Help me. Please help me." He gives her a pitiful look.

Bea sighs. "I'm not your mother, Charlie."

Charlie walks through the front hall of the historic inn. Various staff members greet him by name. He enters the lavish dining room and goes directly to a corner table to join a distinguished-looking older woman. He gives her a peck on the cheek and sits down. He places his napkin in his lap just so and smiles at her.

"Do you notice anything about your place setting?" she says.

Charlie looks at his silverware, plate, water glass, and coffee cup. "No."

"The knife's cutting edge is facing outward. Please fix it."

"Yes, mother."

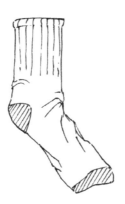

RENNY & SAM

Renny knew that she should pull over. Her head was spinning, and her eyelids felt like stone. She'd already dozed off a couple of times, only to be saved by the thundering crunch of rubber on the back road's gravel shoulder. She'd sworn she wouldn't stop till she reached home, till she could confront Sam before he left for work.

She punched the steering wheel.

When she'd called and that woman answered. She was sure she knew the voice. And here she was being, oh, so nice, doing an errand for Sam, and the bastard was humping some slut. It wasn't the first time, but he kept telling her she was the only one, that he just had a weakness for tight jeans, and he'd promised to change. She thought maybe it was his small dick. She'd heard that guys with small dicks were always trying to prove themselves, that they were real men. She didn't really care. Sex had never been that big of a deal. Sure, it felt good sometimes. She just didn't know what all the fuss was about. Do it and make a baby, like a cow and a bull. But she wasn't ready for that yet. She liked babies some but hated when they cried.

She rolled down the window and stuck out her head. The hot blast took her breath away, and she gasped for air. Reminded her of Sweetie, her black lab, used to do that in the pickup when she and Sam rode out to the ranch early mornings.

What was it with Sam? she wondered. They'd been sweethearts since high school. He'd been the first and only to get in her pants, and they got married the day after graduation. She was proud of her diploma and still had it in a kitchen drawer somewhere. Pulled an all-nighter to Reno, both of them drunk when they said "I do" in the Elvis Chapel, Elvis himself delivering the vows. They'd danced down the empty aisle to the tune of "Don't Be Cruel".

Renny's mouth tasted like garbage. She reached down between her legs to grab the vodka bottle and swerved off the road. She spun the wheel but too late and skidded down a slight incline onto the barren plain, taking a barbed wire fence with her. Dust swirled around and into the car.

She rubbed her eyes. "Shit."

She tipped the vodka bottle to her lips and squeezed out the last drop. I'll cut off his goddamn balls, she thought, tossing the empty bottle out the window.

She stumbled out and looked at the damage. The wire had raked itself down one side, but other than that, the old Chevy was okay. Nothing a little primer wouldn't fix. Then she saw the flat tire. Kicked it.

"So what if I drink," she said. "You'd fucking drink, too, if you had to put up with this bullshit."

The headlights filtered through the settling dust. It was curious, she thought, how the light went on and on and then just stopped till you couldn't see past it. Like it had hit a black wall.

Bathed in the headlight beam, she walked away from the car, her hands swimming before her. I'll reach the end and see what's there, she thought. Maybe I can touch it—the end of light! She laughed. She tried to remember something about the speed of light, something she'd learned in school, about how the sun rays that hit the earth were already a week old, or something.

She stopped after about a quarter mile and looked back toward the car. The headlights stared back at her, like the eyes of a wildcat, waiting. Her hands glowed from the soft, distant light. She really missed Sissy. She didn't really blame Sam for running her over.

Hell, she bolted right out in front of them. No one could've stopped in time. But she didn't like the way he buried her, stuffing her in a garbage bag and taking her to the dump. She'd wanted to bury her in the backyard, but Sam had told her that was a stupid idea, that all the dogs in the neighborhood would come and dig her up.

"I loved that dog, you asshole," she said to the dark.

She wasn't sure if Sam's thing was really too small, but most times, they had trouble putting their parts together. They were usually drunk too, so maybe that was some of the problem. She did know that his was about half the size of her older brother's. She'd walked in on him one day when they were teenagers as he was getting out of the shower. It didn't matter now, anyhow. Hell, maybe she wouldn't ever go back. Sam had tricked her this time, and she didn't like that. He'd sent her on a wild goose chase for some "special" part for his stupid jalopy he ran in the demolition derbies. Two hours of driving, after work, no less, and the guy had told her the part had been sold a week ago and that Sam knew about it.

She'd needed a drink before heading home. Just needed a little time to cool down. She was mad at Sam, but maybe he'd just made a mistake. But that damn giggling bitch on the phone when she'd called him from the bar to tell him she'd be late. He had told her that Judy—yes, that was her name, the little slut who used to follow Sam around in high school—that she'd gotten a flat tire right in front of their house, and he was helping her fix it, and she'd just come in to get a drink of water. And it hadn't helped when the drunk hanging off her in the bar pinched her butt. But he didn't stick around after she kicked him in the shin with her pointy-toed cowboy boot.

The grit in her mouth felt like sandpaper on her tongue. She wanted to spit but couldn't work up the saliva. She spit anyway. I won't go home tonight, she thought. That'll show him. She raised her arms and spun around.

"I won't go home, I won't go home till morning," she sang as she twirled.

She twirled faster and faster, singing and twirling until she vomited and fell to the ground. Just a little nap, and then I'll go home, she thought. She wiped the drool from her chin.

A dull, throbbing pain in her head woke Renny. She opened her eyes. It was pitch black except for the few stars that offered little light. She ran her tongue around her sticky, dry mouth, sat up, and rubbed her face. She swiveled this way and that. Struggled to her feet.

"You said the battery was almost new. Another lie, you bastard."

She squinted into the darkness, trying to get her bearings. I didn't walk that far, she thought. Can't be too hard to find. Course, I'll have to fix the flat.

When Renny didn't show up by morning, Sam got in his pickup and headed out. He knew that she would take the back roads home, always trying to avoid the law.

He spotted her old Chevy when he was about a half mile away. Tumbleweed bounced off it in the freshening breeze.

He walked toward the car, calling out Renny's name, searching the horizon for any sign. He bent down, picked up the empty vodka bottle, and then headed off, following her boot tracks in the billowing dust.

WRONG NUMBER

The incessant ring of the hotel fire alarm rouses Maggie from a deep sleep. She crawls out of bed and reaches for the doorknob. It falls off in her hand. Smoke seeps in under the door. She runs to the window, each step as though she were stuck in honey. But the window isn't a window, only a painting depicting a bucolic neon scene. The ringing, ringing. She clamps her hands over her ears. I'm going to die, and I'm naked, she thinks. Then wakes up.

Maggie opens her eyes and gropes for the portable phone ringing on her bedside table. The red glow of the alarm clock reads 2:10.

"Hello?"

"Yo."

"Yo? Who's this?"

"It's me, you idiot."

"I'm sorry. Who?"

The line goes dead. Maggie feels around in the dark and plunks the phone back in its cradle. I hate calls in the middle of the night, she thinks and drifts off.

The phone rings. Maggie flips on the light and grabs the phone.

"Hello?"

"I made it."

"What?"

103

"I'm here."

"To whom am I speaking?"

"Brett, you moron."

Maggie can hear loud voices in the background. "I'm afraid you have the wrong number ... again."

"Oops. My bad."

"Your English is terrible."

"I gotta go."

"Wait, don't hang up," Maggie says.

"What?"

"You've woken me up, so we might as well talk."

Brett laughs. "Really, I gotta go."

"Young man, you owe it to me. I won't be able to get back to sleep for hours, and tomorrow I'll be a mess. I'm giving you a chance to atone for your mistake."

I'm really sorry for waking you, but I'm at a party."

"You saved my life," Maggie says.

"What?"

"I was having a bad dream when you called. My hotel was burning down, and I couldn't escape."

"Oh yeah, I've had dreams like that. Well, not exactly. It's usually some monster chasing me," Brett says.

"I'm assuming you're young," Maggie says.

"Why?"

"Your horrid lingo, for starters. And monster dreams are wasted on the young. When you're older, they get more sophisticated, like trying to fly."

"Cool. What are you, a shrink?"

Maggie laughs. "I'm a mother."

"Well, good guess, mom. I'm twenty-two. But really, I gotta go."

"Brett, wait. You also scared me to death. I could have had a heart attack."

"No way."

"When you have five grown children and four grandchildren and get a call in the middle of the night, you always think something terrible has happened."

"Sorry, I didn't know. I mean, it was a wrong number, right?"

"Correct, but still."

"Can't you talk to your husband? Or is he sleeping?"

"He's dead."

"Oh. Sorry again."

"It's okay. He was a jerk. Anyway, you're all I have right now."

There's a moment of silence at both ends of the line.

"What's your name?" Brett asks.

"Margaret, but you can call me Maggie."

"So, you must be old, Maggie."

Maggie laughs. "Why do you say that?"

"Your husband's dead? You have grandchildren?"

Maggie clears her throat. "A lady never divulges her age."

Brett laughs. "Like I said, old. But I bet you're still good-looking."

"Go on."

"It's the tone of your voice. I'm a musician, a singer. I can tell."

"Well, thank you, Brett. I consider myself fairly attractive. Not movie star quality, of course, but I can still turn some heads on the street."

Someone shouts something indecipherable near Brett's phone. Brett laughs.

"What was that?" Maggie says.

Brett doesn't respond.

"Brett? Are you still there?" She hears the sound of exhaling. "Brett?"

"Hi, Maggie."

"Thought I'd lost you. What's going on?"

He laughs.

"Are you smoking pot?"

"How'd you guess?"

"Brett, dear. Five children?"

"Right."

"Do you mind if I smoke?" Maggie says.

"A joint?"

"A cigarette. Though I have smoked pot."

"No way." Brett takes another toke.

Maggie smiles. "Good for sex."

Smoke explodes from Brett's mouth. He erupts in a coughing frenzy.

"Jesus, Maggie. You didn't have to tell me that."

"Why not? We're being honest here, aren't we?"

"I thought I was just keeping you company."

Maggie lights a cigarette and inhales. "Let's get serious, Brett." Smoke drifts out of the corners of her mouth. "Why did you call me at two in the morning?"

"Huh? I didn't call you. It was a wrong number, remember?"

"I'm not senile. Who were you calling and why at such an ungodly hour?" Maggie takes another drag and closes her eyes.

Brett's end is silent.

"Brett? Answer me."

"It's really none of your business, Maggie."

"Don't be rude, and please call me Margaret from now on."

"You're starting to sound a little pathetic ... Margaret."

"And you're beginning to sound like a son of a bitch ... Brett."

Brett laughs. "So, when did you first realize you hated men?"

"Why, you ungrateful little bastard," Maggie yells into the phone. "This is the last time I'm ever going to talk to you." She hangs up and stubs out her cigarette. Glares at the ceiling.

The phone rings. Maggie answers it but doesn't speak.

"I'm sorry, Margaret."

Maggie lets out a long, slow breath.

"I am, too, Brett. You can call me Maggie."

"I have to go now, Maggie. Party and all."

"I understand. Thanks for calling, Brett."

"No problem."

"Call any time," Maggie says.

They both hang up.

Maggie lights a cigarette and inhales. She coughs. The smoke comes out in bursts. "Terrible habit," she says and puts out the cigarette. She flips off the light, nestles into her pillow, and closes her eyes. Seconds later, she lets out a huge sigh and turns on the light. Punches the Caller ID button on her phone. Dials. Someone picks up.

"Yo."

"It's me."

Brett laughs. "You must have the wrong number."

"I know you're kidding, but I can't get to sleep."

"I can't talk now, Maggie. I was just about to sing."

"Oh ... Can I listen?"

"Uh ... Okay."

"Oh, goody. You've made an old lady happy, Brett."

"A 'good-looking' old lady."

Maggie beams and runs her fingers through her hair. "Brett?"

"Yes?"

"You don't sing that terrible rock and roll stuff, do you?"

Brett laughs. "I'll sing you a lullaby."

Maggie smiles. "You're a good boy, Brett."

"Sweet dreams, Maggie."

COLD WINTER MORNING

Colin stepped out his front door into the cold winter morning. The sky was a robin's egg blue. His nostrils flared with a deep inhale of the frigid air. Snow-covered meadows stretched down the valley below. Naked tree branches coated with ice shimmered in the bright sun.

Clamping on his snowshoes, Colin marched up the mountain behind his house. He knew that after reaching the summit, which would take about an hour, it was a short downhill ramble before reaching Stone Point, overlooking Hidden Lake, his final destination. He had made the trip many times over the years, and it was one of his favorite treks.

Colin's snowshoes broke through the thin-crusted snow, a few inches of fresh powder on top from last night's flurries. He heard a blue jay's strident squawk followed by the rhythmic chatter of a chickadee. Ascending through the pine forest, he caught the scent of resin. The rising mist vanished into the warming sun. He stopped for a moment to rest. His billowing white breath enveloped his flushed face. Everything was still. Quiet.

Continuing on, Colin felt his heart pump with the exertion. His arms and legs responded to the increasing incline, the motion and rhythm of the climb, synchronizing with the effort. He smiled. A fine day to be alive, he thought.

Colin had decided a week ago to end his life. Two recent events had convinced him that it was the right thing to do. The first involved a skiing accident, which resulted in the tragic death of a teenage boy, a family friend. The boy's mother had eloquently and convincingly stated at the funeral that her son "would be eighteen forever, and when we were all old and feeble, he would still be young and vital." The enticing idea of remaining the same age at the time of one's death throughout eternity intrigued Colin—evoking fantasies of Peter Pan and youthful immortality.

The other deciding factor took place at a concert given by the local youth orchestra. Colin was on the verge of tears during most of the performance, swept away by the youthful energy and innocent yet powerful expression of the musical classics. Afterward, in the dim lobby with his wife, son, and daughter, trying to decide where to go for dinner, a stooped old man escorted by a younger woman shuffled by. With a crook in his flamingo neck, the old man stared ahead with vacant eyes. The skin on his ashen face was drawn tight, lips pulled back in a grimace over gums and teeth. He wore a gray fedora, a long gray coat with black velvet lapels, and grasped an ebony cane with an etched silver tip. Quite an elegant picture, Colin thought, but not an inspiring one. The sight of the old man made him nauseous. He sat down to regain his composure.

Colin's wife asked him what the problem was. He mumbled something about being hungry, but, in reality, he had felt the frailty in the old man's body and seen death in the old man's face. He sensed great unhappiness in the old man, whose life, because of advancing years, had seemingly lost all of its pleasure. Colin did not want to die like that. He wanted to die while he was still a vital human being—to be remembered by his family and friends as "one full of life."

Colin snagged a snowshoe on a buried limb. He fell forward, and his face hit the ground. The cold snow on his hot skin brought him back to the moment. Twisting his head, he recognized a massive rock formation and knew he wasn't far from the summit. It wouldn't be long before he stood on the cliff face above Hidden Lake, overlooking the rocks and water below.

Colin knew it was a selfish decision, but the older he got, the more fearful he became, not only of old age and death but of being remembered as a senile, incontinent, pathetic old man. His own mother had died at the age of fifty-two, and he remembered her, in spite of her debilitating disease, as a woman still lively and fresh.

Colin wanted to be remembered as he was on this day, at age forty-nine, in the prime of his life. He was still in good shape, having kept physically and mentally active. He was a responsible, loving father and husband, an active community member, a musician, a composer of some renown, and overall well-liked and respected by his peers. He didn't think it could get any better than this, and for some time now, he had been getting little indications that he was going downhill. His memory was starting to go ever so slightly, and the index and pinky fingers of his left hand were showing signs of early arthritis—not good for playing the violin or guitar. The degenerative process had set in, and he was beginning the inexorable slide toward disintegration and death. He had reached a point when progress or improvement, even with very hard work, would be impossible or negligible at best. He had always measured his growth as a human being by the positive results of countless hours of practice and disciplined concentrated effort, and for a while now, it hadn't been happening.

Colin picked himself up from the snow bank and trudged onward. A breeze carried the fresh smell of earth and forest. Taking a deep breath, a sweet, soothing balm entered his lungs—a hint of spring in the air. Just the other day, he had heard a phoebe call its name in the woods, seen the flash of a robin's red breast.

Colin didn't think he would be sorely missed. His two children were out of college and seemed to be firmly grounded in their endeavors. His wife of twenty-five years was, above all, a practical woman and, after the initial shock, would soon realize the wisdom behind his decision. She might even follow suit, having expressed many times her dissatisfaction and discomfort with growing old. She couldn't stand the wrinkles on her face and considered getting cosmetic surgery until Colin had talked her out of it. No, he felt strongly that he was doing the right thing. He would be remembered for who he was right now, not as some paralyzed, drooling wheelchair geriatric parked in a rest-home activity room.

Reaching the summit, Colin gazed out over the panorama. Not far below, he could make out the barren ledge of Stone Point and, beyond, cradled in the valley, the ice blue of Hidden Lake. The wind was freshening, focused, and reinforced by the long valley it passed through on its trip north. A red-tailed hawk circled on the thermals above. The southern exposure on this side of the mountain had melted off much of the snow. No further need for snowshoes. Leaning them up against a tree, he started off, quickening his pace on the downhill path.

Within a short time, Colin found himself standing on Stone Point, the large bed of rock overlooking Hidden Lake. The height was dizzying. The cliff face fell for over two hundred feet to the rocks and water below. He inched toward the drop-off, all of a sudden feeling light-headed and timid. He had never been bothered by heights as a youth but discovered, quite accidentally, that he had grown fearful of them. He was working on his house one day, repairing the roof. He hadn't paid much attention as he climbed the ladder, but when he straddled the ridge cap and eased closer to the edge, he realized that he felt out of control. Afraid he would just fall off or, worse yet, have the uncontrollable urge to jump. This aversion had only grown stronger with age and was just another sign of approaching decay.

Colin stood as still as possible, but the strengthening breeze challenged his balance. He looked at the water below, crashing over the rocks and onto the shore. It seemed to be calling, beckoning to him—one of Odysseus's Sirens. He fixed his gaze on an outcropping of rocks. The bulky formation glistened with a golden umber in the bright sunlight. The surf's spray had frozen around its base, creating a delicate transparent skirt of fine, icy lace.

He closed his eyes and listened. He couldn't tell if he was hearing the rustle of the trees in the wind, the lapping surf, or the blood rushing through his veins. It was white noise, indistinct and pervasive. And confining. He felt imprisoned by the sibilant reverberations and screamed just to hear something else. And as he screamed, he leaned forward on the balls of his feet. The wind was picking up in velocity, and he could feel its building pressure pressing on his torso. He felt suspended in time, secure, as the wind held him in place. Raising his arms as if to do a swan dive, he opened his watery eyes and glanced out over the vista of now shimmering colors—the rich coniferous greens, distant mountain grays, effervescent snow whites, and the clear blue waters of Hidden Lake. He looked down at the rocks below, nestled in shards of shredded ice that reflected the sun's brilliant rays. He had leaned far enough into the wind that he had reached the critical angle of no return—an irretrievable angle from which the only direction of movement was downward. He tried to jump out as if to escape upwards like Icarus soaring toward the sun, but as soon as his feet left the ledge, he plummeted head first like a stone. He drew his arms close to his side—a human arrow hurtling toward a violent, sudden end. In an instant, he would strike eternity's bull's eye. It was at this precise moment that Colin realized exactly what it was that made life so precious.

MAUDE & LYMAN GO SOUTH

Maude, my wife of twenty-five years, was a kind soul and never meant any harm, but sometimes she'd get stuck on a subject and wouldn't let it go. Since I'd been laid off at the lumber yard last fall, her focus lately was on "potential" and, having birthed five children had fulfilled hers. At least, I thought she had.

Being in my fifties, I figured I'd exhausted any potential I might have exhibited growing up. But she'd harp on me about my music. True, I'd been a decent musician when I was younger. Done some professional gigs, in bars, at flea markets, busking, and whatnot. Even had dreams of being "discovered" and playing for a big audience, everyone shouting out my name. But my hearing had dulled over the years and some of my joints weren't working as best they could. I wasn't inspired to hop back on a flea-bitten nag.

It was early March in Vermont, and I was moping around the house, something I liked to do near the end of a long winter. Maude said I'd feel better about myself if I got a job. She always seemed to have an answer for all of my problems.

I was debating the pros and cons of investing our remaining life savings on a week at a poker academy, success guaranteed, when the phone rang. It was an old buddy who'd moved to Key West. He said, "Come on down and relax. A friend of mine has a condo, and will be out of town for a week. You can stay there for free." I didn't like to travel much, and I've never been a good tourist. Must have been all those years holed up in Vermont. But free was a refreshing word, and Maude loved a bargain. Besides, she got me when she said, "Lyman if we don't get out of here, you're going to drive me crazy."

I'm not saying Key West wasn't an interesting place. We did visit the Little White House, and I might've even touched Harry

Truman's poker table except for the quick reflexes of our tour guide. But the main drag was like something out of a bad dream.

You could spend any time day or night gawking at the scantily clad college coeds stumbling up and down the sleazy strip, drinks in hand, marveling at the curious beauty of the transvestites, or even get a picture taken with a giant banana snake draped around your neck (why would anyone want to do that?). I won't mention the seedy establishments with women standing outside in their underwear trying to lure innocent young men. But I was from New England, with strong Puritan blood, so sitting in the condo eating frozen dinners and watching TV suited me just fine.

We'd only been there three days when Maude's shadow fell over me as I reclined on the couch, comfortable and cool in my favorite Hawaiian shirt.

"I'm bored," she said.

"Okay," I said.

"I'm going for a walk."

I checked my watch. "It's two o'clock."

"Don't worry. I'll be home by six. Wouldn't want to upset your dinner routine."

I straightened up. That last comment had a little bite to it. "Is there something wrong, button?"

"I'm fine. See you later." With that, she was out the door.

Telling me that she was "fine" bothered me a bit. She was hardly ever "fine," but I decided not to worry and took a nap.

The phone rang and pulled me out of a peaceful and dreamless sleep.

"Hello?"

"Hey, Lyman."

I was pretty sure it was Maude, but she sounded strange.

"Maude? You okay?"

"Never felt better in my life."

This was odd. Used to be it was our wedding day. "Where are you?"

"Booty Hill."

A chorus of raucous voices chimed in behind her, "Bar and Grill!"

A shiver ran through me. "What? That's on that street. You better come home," I said. "Besides, I'm hungry."

"Oh no, Lyman, I'm having too much fun."

This was worrisome. Maude was a serious person. She rarely had time for fun. But maybe this was just what she needed.

"Okay," I said. "I'll fix a TV dinner. See you later."

Her end of the phone went dead. I shrugged, figuring she was a grown woman and could take care of herself. I was halfway through cooking supper in the microwave when it dawned on me, the sign flashing through my mind, "Booty Hill Bar & Grill – Clothing Optional." No, that couldn't be it. Must've been "Optional Clothing." Or was it? I ran out the door.

The Strip was only a couple of blocks away, and I jogged as fast as my bad knees would take me. I found the Booty Hill sign, and the picture of a topless woman at a bar talking to a bare-assed man confirmed my suspicion. I huffed and puffed up the outside staircase. I guess you wouldn't want to just stumble off the street into an establishment like this.

A bouncer at the door, a transvestite with muscles to boot, said the cover charge was a piece of clothing. I offered him a crisp ten-dollar bill. He waved me to the side and let in a couple that had followed up behind me. They had no trouble taking something off. I sighed, handed him my favorite Hawaiian shirt, sucked in my ample belly, hiked up my pants, and marched through the door.

The odors of old sweat, stale beer, and cigar smoke about knocked me over. And I had to blink several times just to make sure I was seeing correctly. The place was jammed wall-to-wall with bodies in various stages of undress. And it was loud! Boisterous laughter at the bar, dancers singing along with a nude guitar player belting out a country and western song. Had to admit, he was wearing a smart-looking cowboy hat.

I scanned the crowd but couldn't spot Maude. She was always accusing me, and rightly so, of not paying attention to what she was wearing. But I sure as hell was paying attention now to what she might *not* be wearing.

I decided to take matters into my own hands. "Maude!" I bellowed. The place fell dead silent. I guess she had made some friends.

"Let'im through, boys."

The crowd parted like the Red Sea. She was lying face up on a table, topless, with a shot glass balanced in her cleavage. Her head dangled over the edge. A bald, naked man stood over her. If I wasn't mistaken, he looked like he was shaking salt on one of her breasts.

"Hey, baldy," I shouted. "Back off!"

He turned and looked me up and down. "Get in line, gramps."

"Yeah," someone in the crowd shouted. "We paid good money for this."

It was then that I noticed the bills stuck in the waistband of Maude's panties.

"For what, exactly?" I said to the crowd.

A chinless man with thick glasses and a hairy chest stepped forward. "Lick salt and lime off her tits, then with your hands behind your back, try and drink the shot of tequila. Called the 'Oasis Special.'"

"What's 'oasis' got to do with it?" I said.

Chinless Man held out his hands like two upside-down cups. "Well, you have two sand dunes, and right between them—"

"All right, I get the picture." I stomped up to Maude, nudging the bald guy to the side. "Let's go," I said to her.

"You look funny upside down," she said.

The bald man hip-checked me out of the way, put his hands behind his back, and leaned over Maude.

I snatched the shot glass off Maude's chest and downed it. "I'll be the only one drinking from my wife's oasis."

The crowd cheered.

"You go, Lyman!" Maude screeched.

The guitar player struck up a tune. Someone handed me another shot, and I downed it. Maude stood up and grabbed me. "Let's dance."

"You know I don't dance," I said. "Let's find your clothes and get out of here."

She wriggled in a way I'd never seen her do at home. "C'mon, Lymie, live a little."

I grabbed her hand to make for the exit, but a crowd had formed a circle around us.

Maude made a sad face. "Lymie says he can't dance."

"Awe," the crowd said.

"But he can play the guitar!" she said.

"Ooooh," the crowd chorused. "Lymie, Lymie."

I was swept off my feet and passed hand-over-hand until I landed on the stage. Maude followed me up. The guitar player hung his guitar around my neck and plopped the cowboy hat on my head. It was just my size.

"Join the party and drop trou, gramps," someone shouted.

Maude mouthed something to the crowd.

"What'd you say?" I asked.

"She says you go 'commando,'" a buxom lady called out.

The crowd laughed.

"What the hell is that?" I said to Maude.

Maude whispered in my ear. I felt hot blood rushing up my neck. "Gimme another shot," I said. One appeared in my hand, and I slammed it down. Felt the heat in my belly.

I strummed the guitar. Sounded pretty good coming through the electronics.

"Can you sing 'Do Your Balls Hang Low'?" someone hollered.

I grinned, remembering summer camp about forty years back. I adjusted the rake of my hat and leaned into the mic. "Do they wobble to and fro?"

The crowd erupted. "Lymie, Lymie."

I gazed out at my adoring fans, all chanting my name. Then I turned to Maude, the sweet taste of tequila on my lips. "Woman ... drop my pants."

SPECIAL FAVOR

Jane sat in the window seat, admiring the red sun as it disappeared behind the stand of giant maples bordering the backyard. She smiled at the sound of crunching gravel. A midnight blue Mercedes pulled into the driveway.

She greeted Michael at the door with a glass of wine. They went out to the patio and sat next to each other in matching deck chairs.

Michael took a sip of the Merlot. "What's new?"

"I had lunch with Susan at the club," Jane said.

"How's she doing?" he asked, furrowing his brow.

"She hasn't had sex in seven years."

"Jesus, is that what you women talk about? Your sex lives?"

"As if you men don't talk about it in the locker room," she said. "Come on, you can admit it."

Michael gave her a peck on the cheek. "It's between you and me, our little secret. Besides, I don't want to make the boys jealous."

"Liar!" She gave him a friendly slap on the hand. "Promise?"

"Of course," he said. "Did you and Susan come up with a solution? With her situation, it can't be easy." He took a sip of wine.

Jane gave him a sly grin. "I offered your services."

The wine sprayed out of Michael's mouth. "What?"

Jane stroked his wrist. "Under the circumstances, I thought it was the right thing to do."

Michael pulled away. "You want me to fuck my best friend's wife, who, by the way, is your best friend?"

Jane laughed. "Not fuck, dear. Don't be so crude. Make love. She deserves it, and we can provide it."

"We?"

"Yes, we."

"And just where does the 'we' come in?"

"I've made all the arrangements," Susan said, looking at her watch. "She's expecting you at eight."

"Tonight?"

"I'll bet you've thought about it," Jane teased.

"Okay, jokes on me," Michael said and got up. "What's for dinner?"

Jane grabbed his arm and pulled him back down. "Michael, listen to me. I'm serious. Yes, she is my best friend, so I want you to do this. For me." Michael opened his mouth to say something, but Jane pressed a finger to his lips. "Susan is a very sexual being, and she's been deprived of a wonderful experience that we have quite often. I think we should share it. Period."

"You are serious," Michael said. He settled back in his chair and, keeping his eyes on Jane, drained his glass. "Honey, you are one of the most compassionate beings I know. That's one of the reasons I married you. But don't you think this is going a little too far? Our whole relationship is based on trust and fidelity. It's what makes it sexy. You remember what happened to our first marriages?"

"This is different. You know that. Susan needs us now more than ever, and this is one way we can help ease her pain. Now, it's getting late. You'd better freshen up and get over there," she said.

"Forget it. I can't do this to Sam. Call Susan and tell her it's off."

"I don't think Sam will mind. In fact, I think that he'd thank you if he could."

Michael looked down the valley. Shadows cast by the setting sun swept across the rolling meadow below. "How's he doing?"

"You know Jane's given us visiting rights."

Michael poured more wine and took a slug.

Jane sighed. "Michael, it's all right."

"Just tell me, please."

"There's still some slight brain activity," she said. "But it's a million to one that he'll ever recover. And he hasn't moved a muscle in so long that his body has totally atrophied. Susan's thinking of removing him from life-support. Soon."

Michael gave Jane a long look. "This could ruin our marriage."

Jane jumped into Michael's lap and smothered him with kisses. "Oh, thank you, thank you. I knew you'd do it."

"Did you hear me?"

Jane kissed him again. "Honey, we are soul mates. There is absolutely nothing that could pull us apart. Besides, we're doing a wonderful favor for our dearest friend who can't remember ever having a normal life. It's a noble cause." She jumped off his lap and bowed. "My hero ... duty calls."

Michael fidgeted on the front porch of the secluded, elegant country home. The door burst open. Susan, a dark-haired woman in her late thirties, a burgundy shift accentuating the curves of her athletic, supple body, gave Michael a big smile.

"You're on time," she said.

"Wouldn't want to be late on the first date," he said as she beckoned him in.

They sat down on either end of the living room couch. On the coffee table were two wine glasses, one half-full, and a near-empty bottle of wine. Through the French doors, Michael could see the flower garden in the backyard he and Jane had helped plant. Once abundant and beautiful, it was now a mass of weeds.

"Would you like some wine? I've already had two ... or three." Susan giggled. Michael nodded. She poured, spilling some on the table. "Oops, sorry." She raised her glass to make a toast and froze.

Michael raised his. "To old friends."

"Of course. Why didn't I think of that?"

Their glasses met and made a muted tinkling sound. Susan took a hearty gulp. Michael did the same, then cleared his throat.

"Susan, we've been friends for a long time, but, really, do you think this is the right thing to do?"

Susan frowned. "Oh dear, you don't find me desirable."

"No, no, that's not the point. You are absolutely gorgeous and very, very sexy." Michael touched her arm, which she withdrew.

"Michael, you are such a dear, but seriously, you're right. We don't have to do this," Susan said with a solemn face. "I don't know what Jane and I were thinking. It just seemed like a good idea at the time. I was feeling desperate for some human contact."

"You could call an escort service. It might make things simpler for all of us," Michael said.

"A stranger? I could never do that," Susan said, shaking her head. "No, no, no. What would the neighbors think?"

"You don't have any neighbors."

"Right. Anyway, let's call it off. I can't do this to Jane. I know it was her idea, but she's being too much of a saint."

"As always," Michael said.

They both took a sip of wine and gazed off in opposite directions.

Michael turned back. "I could give you a back rub? To relax you ..."

"And then go home," Susan said.

"Still friends," they said in unison and laughed.

Susan lay down on the Persian carpet in front of the ample stone fireplace. Michael sat down beside her and rubbed her back with one hand.

Susan gave a little moan. "That feels so good. You don't know."

Michael kept kneading, now with both hands.

Susan sighed. "Sam and I had a great sex life."

"So I've heard," Michael said. "Literally."

"Huh?"

"Remember that vacation lodge in Aspen?"

"The one with paper-thin walls?"

They both laughed. Michael pressed down on Susan's back. She gave another moan.

"More," she whispered.

Making no sudden moves, Michael straddled her back and began to massage in earnest. He slid partway down onto her thighs and stroked her lower back. He couldn't help but admire the roundness of her ass. His hands stopped moving.

"Okay, massage over," he said and gave her a quick rub with one hand. "Time to go." He moved to get off her.

"Wait," Susan said, her voice thick.

Michael settled back down on her. "What?"

"Please do me one special favor?"

"If I can."

"Sam used to kiss me very lightly on the back of my neck. It would mean so much to me if you could do that one little thing. Then you can go."

"Sounds reasonable," Michael said. "Just one little kiss."

He parted Susan's dark hair at the nape of her neck. Admired the white and tender skin. She shuddered. He leaned in close. His nostrils twitched at the musky scent. He took a deep breath and then kissed her. She groaned.

Michael stood up, his legs straddling Susan's prone body. She rolled over and stared up at him. He reached out to give her a hand up.

"Party's over," he said with a smile.

She took hold of one of his ankles and caressed it. "I guess Jane never told you."

"What?" Michael gave her a quizzical look.

"Before the accident."

He frowned and glanced away for an instant. "Yes?"

"She slept with Sam."

Susan enjoyed the dumbstruck look on Michael's face.

Michael strode into his bedroom. Jane was in bed reading a book. He went straight for the closet, rummaged around, and pulled out a black carry-on suitcase. Jane sat up.

"Moving out?" she asked playfully. Michael tore a few shirts off hangars and stuffed them in the carry-on. A concerned look passed over her face. "Honey, what's happening? Talk to me."

Michael went to the dresser and yanked open a drawer.

"You didn't ...?" Susan said.

He spun around and glared at her, a pair of socks in his hand. "How could I not?"

Jane grimaced and shook her head. "No, no, no. This wasn't supposed to happen. We just lost a thousand dollars."

Michael clenched the pair of socks. "What are you talking about?"

Jane sighed. "Susan and I had one too many daiquiris at lunch, and I was telling her how faithful you were and that you could never be tempted to sleep with another woman. She bet me that she could entice you into bed. You blew it."

Michael threw the socks at Susan. She ducked, the socks flying past her.

"You fucked Sam!" he shouted.

"What? Don't be ridiculous," she said. "And don't yell at me." She smoothed a wrinkle in the silk sheet. "Now, what are you talking about?"

"Susan told me you and Sam slept together. I don't know when. I thought you might fill me in on the details," Michael said.

Jane motioned for him to sit on the bed, which he did, hanging his head in his hands. She rubbed his back. He flinched.

"Don't touch me," he said.

She withdrew her hand. "Michael, I swear to God, I never slept with Sam."

"I'm going to kill her," Michael said, standing up. "But first, I have something I need to do." He threw a few more pieces of clothing in his carry-on, went into the bathroom and tossed in some toiletries.

"Michael, please come back here," Jane said as he stormed out of the bathroom and through the bedroom door.

Michael stood beside the hospital bed. The heart monitor beeped, its pulsing red wave a faint glow in the dimly lit room. He looked down at the comatose body of his best friend.

"Sam?" Michael whispered. He took hold of a frail hand. "They say hearing's the last to go, so ... I'm sorry about the accident. I should have listened to you and given you the keys, but I was too drunk. I've ruined your life, and I'm going to feel guilty for the rest of mine." He took a deep breath, exhaled. "One more thing ... I just slept with Susan."

A few seconds passed.

Michael felt Sam's fingers twitch.

Michael froze. "Sam?"

Sam's hand squeezed Michael's like a vice. Then went limp.

Michael yanked his hand away as though it had been torched. An incessant whine filled the room. He clamped his hands over his ears, but nothing could keep out the rising wail of the flatline piercing his brain.

GONE TOO FAR

Snowflakes fell on John and Betty as they hurried up the icy stone steps. Betty slipped. John grabbed her arm and steadied her.

"I knew she shouldn't have gone to that party." Betty spits out the words, scowled. "She better have a good excuse. Oh, I feel like such a failure. Our baby."

"I'm sure it's all a misunderstanding," John said. "Don't worry."

He pulled open the heavy wooden door with TOWN POLICE painted in black on the pebbled glass and held it open as Betty passed through.

It was bright inside the waiting area. The couple stopped for a moment to let their night eyes adjust to the cold fluorescent light. An officer sat behind bulletproof glass, sipping coffee and reading a magazine. John motioned Betty to sit down, then went up to the glass partition. He stood looking at the officer, who was too engrossed in the magazine to notice him. John could see that it was a girly magazine. He cleared his throat.

The officer's head snapped up. At the same time, he ditched the magazine under the counter. He flipped open a small flap at the bottom of the partition.

"Can I help you?" the officer asked through the flap.

John leaned down. "We got a message on our answering machine. I've come here to get my daughter, Amy Jones."

"Amy Jones. Right. Uh, you can't see her right now." The officer flipped the flap closed, sat back in his chair, and looked at John. Gave him a sly grin.

John stood there, his gut tightening, but he remained calm on the outside. He tapped on the glass. The officer leaned forward and opened the flap.

"I told you she wasn't ready to see you," the officer said.

John's fists tightened. "You didn't tell me that. You said that I couldn't see her right away. And by the way, can you please tell me why she's here?"

The officer grinned. "You talked to her, didn't you?"

John frowned. Betty came up and asked what the matter was. John motioned her away. Betty eyed the officer, who gave her a lascivious grin. Betty backed off and sat down.

John took a deep breath. "No, I didn't talk to her. Someone here left a message on our answering machine. Now, I'm asking you again. I would like some explanation."

The officer smiled. "You'll get an explanation when I'm ready to give you one. Now go sit down. I'll let you know when she's ready." He slammed the flap shut, got up from his chair, and walked out of view.

"Damn," John blurted. "What the hell is going on here?" He turned to Betty and threw up his hands. "We left the city to get away from this sort of crap, and now we have to deal with this two-bit small-town cop."

"What's the problem, John? Where's Amy?" Betty asked. "I want to see our baby."

John whipped around and put his face up to the glass partition. "Hey! You in there!" he yelled. "I'd like some service!" He banged on the partition with his fist.

The officer came out from around a corner and stood behind the partition, hands in his pockets, twiddling some change.

"What's your name? Where's your name tag?" John yelled.

The officer leaned down and flipped open the flap.

"No need to shout. My name's Officer Brown."

John took a deep breath. "I'd like to speak to the person in charge, someone with real authority around here." He turned to Betty. "I'll get to the bottom of this, dear." He turned back to Officer Brown, who had a gun pointed in his face. John's jaw dropped.

"You want someone in charge? Is that what you want?" Officer Brown waved the gun back and forth in front of John's face. "How's this for being in charge? Meet Officer Killing Machine. You want to talk to Officer Killing Machine? He's in charge."

Officer Brown walked out of sight. John backed away from the partition and over to Betty, who was trembling. John pulled her up by the arm and led her toward the exit. She resisted.

"We can't leave her with these maniacs," she whispered.

"Come with me," John whispered and continued to usher Betty toward the exit. Then, loudly, "We're going to call a lawyer. Take care of this in a civilized manner."

"Hold it right there," Officer Brown shouted. "Down on the floor, on your stomachs, hands behind your heads."

John and Betty spun around.

Officer Brown, two feet away, motioned with his gun. "Down. Now. Or I'll blast a hole between your eyes."

John pulled Betty down to the floor. She began to sob.

"Put your hands behind your head," John hissed at her. She did.

Officer Brown stood over them and holstered his gun. Gave a half-laugh. "Just messin' with you. But watch your step. We 'two-bit small-town cops' ain't deaf. Get up. I'll go get Amy."

Betty was about to say something, but John cupped his hand over her mouth and shook his head. He stood and helped Betty to her feet.

"Can they do this?" she whispered.

"Apparently," John replied as he brushed the dust from his jacket.

The door to the office swung open, and Officer Brown led Amy out, her dress torn and dirty, her face covered with a bandage. Only her eyes were visible. Betty and John ran over and hugged her.

John looked accusingly at Officer Brown. "What in God's name happened to her?"

"She was in a little accident, but the doctor released her, so I guess she'll be fine once the drugs wear off." Officer Brown smiled. "Except for the hit-and-run charges."

Betty took hold of Amy's left hand and looked curiously at a gold band on her finger. "Amy? Where did you get this ring?"

Amy, with a muffled sob, pulled her hand away and snapped her head back and forth. Betty stepped back, looked Amy over, and then turned to John.

"This isn't Amy," Betty said.

"What? What are you talking about?" John said.

Betty glared at Officer Brown. "These are not her clothes, and," she turned to John, "our daughter is not married, in case you didn't know."

John turned on Officer Brown. "What are you trying to pull, you asshole? Dragging us down here for this bullshit!" He lunged at Officer Brown, knocking them both to the floor. He pounded his fists into Officer Brown's face as Betty grabbed him from behind to pull him off.

"Stop it John, stop! It's all just a horrible mistake!" Betty screamed.

Officer Brown yanked his gun from its holster. John grabbed Officer Brown's gun hand and twisted. The gun went off. The bullet pierced Officer Brown right between the eyes.

John, wide-eyed, dropped the gun. Blood from the hole in Officer Brown's head spurted all over the front of John's jacket.

"What have you done, John?" What have you done?" Betty screamed.

John struggled to his feet, shaken. He grabbed Betty and yanked her toward the exit.

They burst out the heavy wooden door, keeping an eye on it as they stumbled backward down the icy steps.

A young woman walked up the steps toward them. "Mom? Dad?"

John and Betty spun around.

"Amy? Oh, Amy," Betty wailed and fell into her daughter's arms. "What are you doing here?"

Amy brushed the tear-stained hair out of her mother's eyes. "I heard the message on the answering machine. I had to laugh when the cop said that they 'had Amy.' I assumed they'd caught the girl who stole my wallet at the party. I hope you weren't too worried." She looked at her father. Cocked her head. "Dad?"

John stared at his daughter.

"What's that all over your jacket?" she said.

THE ROACH

I'm going to tell you a story about a friend who's no longer with us. His name was Joey "The Roach" Evans. It begins in the seventies when we were around twelve-years-old living in a rundown Brooklyn tenement. Along with our derelict parents, there were some rats, but the roaches were rampant.

Joey wasn't allowed any pets, so he bonded with the roaches. And because I liked Joey—he was different from the other kids who usually wanted to use me as a punching bag—I also ended up spending time with the roaches.

Once, I went over to his apartment and found him sitting on the kitchen floor, roaches crawling all over him.

"If you don't move, they think you're just another piece of furniture," Joey said. He plucked one off his arm and, with little fanfare, bit off its head and spit it out.

I shrieked.

Joey laughed. "Not to worry. It can live for a week without its head."

"You're strange in the head," I said, backing away.

"Try it," Joey said. He held a roach toward me, pinched between his thumb and forefinger. "Take this one and bite off its head."

"Forget it," I said, almost to the door.

"If you don't do it, you're not my friend," he said.

I sighed. He had me there. I gingerly took the roach from Joey. They weren't particularly cuddly, to begin with, so if you've ever held a large, six-legged squirmy insect intending to bite off its head, maybe you know how I felt. After five unhappy seconds, I threw the

137

thing across the room. It hit the wall, fell to the floor, and scurried toward me. I ran out.

A week later, I was, leaning against an old corrugated shed in the abandoned lot across the street, reading a comic featuring my favorite character, the Silver Samurai. I loved his super-powered Katana sword! Joey appeared, and we stood there for a while, kicking at the dust.

"I'd sure like a samurai sword," I said.

"Maybe with that, you could manage to cut off a roach's head," Joey scoffed.

I ignored his comment, although I thought he's right, and it would be a swift, sure cut!

"I'd sure like a soda right about now," I said.

"Not me," Joey said. "I can go for months without fluids."

"Can't," I said. "Only camels can do that."

"Actually, that's not true," Joey said. "Rats can go a lot longer without water than a camel."

"Yeah," I said, pawing at the dirt with my sneaker. "I knew that. You know what else?" Joey gave me a quizzical look. "I think rats are going to take over the world. Did you know they can chew through lead?"

Joey doubled over with laughter. "You are one dumb-ass. Roaches are going to take over the world. Did you know they could survive an atomic blast? Huh? Did you know that, wise guy?"

I stared at the ground and shuffled my feet.

"And I heard you can put one in a microwave, and it won't even flinch, no matter how long you cook it," Joey said.

I sprung to attention. We had a microwave. "Bet'cha it can't."

I'd rarely seen Joey so excited. We took a roach over to my parents' apartment and stuck it in the microwave for one minute. We watched through the glass as the roach tore around the interior, doing frequent summersaults and backflips. When the timer went off, we opened the door, and the roach scampered out. Joey caught it, put it back in the microwave, and set the timer at ten minutes. That roach put on quite a show, worthy of a circus act, an acrobat on speed, but, in the end, it crept out of the microwave under its own power, though a tad bit slower than before. Impressed, we let it crawl up the wall and disappear into a crack. I gained a new respect for roaches that day. They were true survivors. A creature we could learn from.

Ten years passed. I'd spent some time in Juvee detention centers.

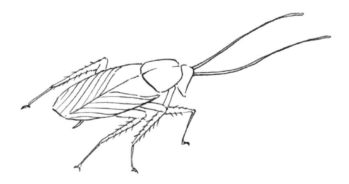

Remember that microwave? It turns out it wasn't mine, along with many other appliances the cops found in our apartment. More recently, I'd hung six months in the Pen for some simple thing like hotwiring a car and taking it for a joy ride. For all my failings, I'd always been mechanically inclined.

When I got out, I had no place to go, so I thought I'd look up Joey at the old tenement. I knocked on his door but got no answer. I tried the latch, and the door opened. I fell back, overwhelmed by a terrible stench. I held my nose and walked in. I found Joey at the kitchen stove, hovering over a big boiling pot.

"What the hell are you cooking?" I squeaked through my clamped nose.

"This is a concoction that will save the human race," Joey said, stirring the pot with a huge ladle, an intent look on his face. "Almost done."

"I'd like to stay for dinner, but I have some important place to go," I said.

"We're not going to eat this. We're gonna shoot it," Joey said, removing the pot from the stove. "Look at this stuff. Isn't it great?"

I was confused. I might have done some crazy things growing up with Joey, but we had never done drugs, hard ones, anyway. I peeked into the pot of brown, simmering liquid with unnamable objects floating on top and recoiled. "Man, that looks disgusting. What is it?"

"Roach stew," Joey said. "Remember back when we were kids and put that roach in the microwave?"

I nodded.

"They're indestructible, right?"

I nodded again.

"Well, I've created the first roach serum, and, lucky for you showing up at this very moment, we're going to be the first humans to inject it." He gave me a triumphant smile. "Don't you get it? This is our ticket out of here! We're gonna be invincible! Supermen! And rich, rich, rich!"

As was my usual response to Joey's roach madness, I started backing out of the room. "I don't stick needles into my body. Why don't we just smoke a joint?"

Joey sighed. "O.K., if you're gonna be such a chicken shit, at least hang and make sure everything goes all right. Can you do that for me ... friend?"

What could I do? I watched as Joey sucked some of the gross, brown, foul-smelling liquid into a syringe (easy to find around the tenement), pulled down his pants—I turned away, he was so out of shape—injected himself in the butt, and passed out.

He woke up about twenty-four hours later complaining of a terrible thirst and drank a gallon of water.

"Roaches can die of thirst in one week," he said.

"You're not a roach," I said.

"Let's see," he said. "Time me."

"What?"

He smirked. "Roaches can hold their breath for forty minutes."

He handed me his wristwatch, held his breath, and leaned back against the fridge. I kept one eye on Joey and the other on the watch. After what seemed forever, Joey's lungs burst, and he sucked in some air.

"How'd I do?" he gasped.

"You're not quite there yet. Only thirty-seven minutes," I said, sure that he would now give up this madness.

Joey pumped his fist. "Yes!" He jumped up and ran circles around me, picking up speed with each rotation. I got dizzy watching him. He finally collapsed in a heap. "Roaches are also incredibly

141

fast for an insect and, as you can see, I am too, for a human. It's all relative," he got out between breaths.

"If you say so," I said, still trying to clear my dizzy head. "Well, I think I'd better be—"

He held up his hand and stared at me through his thick spectacles. "Next test. You're gonna build me a microwave."

I shot him a look. "It'd be easier to steal one."

He shook his head back and forth. "No, no, no. A giant microwave. One I can climb into. Don't you get it? If I'm really part cockroach, I'll be able to survive a microwave and, expanding my hypothesis, survive a nuclear blast—making me invincible. This is where the money comes in. Any government on the planet will pay megabucks to own the rights to this serum. And, believe me, the bidding will be high." He was frothing at the mouth.

"I don't know how to build a microwave," I said.

"You can rebuild a 350 c.c. Ford Fairlane, can't cha?"

"Well, duh," I said. "I could really hop the carb on that one."

"Well then, I have the original plans for the very first microwave. It was six feet tall and weighed about a three-quarter ton. I ought to fit in that."

Without boring you with the mundane details of constructing a giant microwave, I completed it in a couple of weeks. The plans were fairly simple, and our neighborhood had plenty of junkyards. And Joey had become incredibly strong—he was a big help carrying almost a ton of material up the five flights of stairs.

We set the microwave up in his living room. Joey handed me his glasses. "We know metal explodes in a microwave."

"Right," I said. "How about fillings?"

Joey scowled. "Unlike you, piss breath, I floss."

My mouth snapped shut. I had a lot of cavities, even a missing tooth. Prison dentistry wasn't a top priority for taxpayers. He turned to enter the microwave. I gave him a quick once-over.

"Belt!" I cried out.

Joey paused in mid-step, turned, and smiled at me. "You're starting to think like a roach." He undid his buckle and smoothly pulled the belt through the loops.

Boy, did I admire this guy's panache. He flipped the belt into a corner, gave me a crisp salute, and stepped into the microwave. "See you on the other side," he said as I slammed the heavy door shut and secured it.

I could see Joey through the glass window in the microwave door. He sat down on the little wooden bench I had built for him, using only dowels to fasten it (we *had* thought of everything).

Joey gave me the thumbs-up. I wound the old-fashioned kitchen timer to our prearranged goal of ten minutes. That's what the roach had survived and we now considered ourselves on their level. I flipped the switch and sat back to watch. I would turn off the microwave if Joey pounded three times on the glass. Under no circumstance should I make any decisions as to his well-being. That was fine with me.

As I watched Joey, the first thing I noticed, besides the annoying tick-tick-tick of the timer, was that his eyes started to bulge out of his head. It sure looked painful, but he pressed them back in with his fists and gave me another thumbs-up. He started to wriggle and then to shake but still managed to smile at me. What a trooper!

At five minutes, Joey was doing back flips, which was very impressive, him being pudgy and unathletic. With two minutes left,

Joey pressed his face to the glass, which he clawed at with his fingers. He convulsed. Drool slid down the window. But I held my ground. I wasn't going to screw up our future.

The dinger finally went off. I lunged for the switch and flipped open the latch. The microwave door flew open, and Joey fell out onto the floor. His ears were smoking and eyes clamped shut. Other than that, he seemed okay. I slapped him around a bit to get the blood circulating (he'd taught me that in our run-through). His eyelids fluttered open, his dry, cracked lips parted. "We did it," he whispered.

Joey spent the next several months trying to sell the roach serum to the highest bidder. The problem was he couldn't find any. He wasn't a real people-person, to begin with, and it didn't help that he had developed a foul-smelling body odor that no amount of deodorant could disguise. He was particularly proud of this, one more indication of his budding "roach-ness."

I was with him when he tried to convince some local businessmen to buy into his scheme. He told them that, besides surviving a nuclear blast, he could climb their office walls with his bare hands (after several more injections, he had developed small roach-like claws on his fingers and toes). When that didn't go too well—the walls were glass—he begged them to come with us and observe the microwave test. They laughed us out of there.

Joey was upset. When we got back to the apartment, he held his breath for forty-one minutes and passed out. When he came to, I told him his time.

He punched a hole in the wall. "I declare myself 'Roach Supreme.'"

"You da Roach," I said.

After running circles around me one day, something he was now prone to do quite often (he told me it was his way of "thinking"), he said that he had the answer to all our problems, which, at this point, were mounting due to lack of money and little food. We had managed to make some spare change on the streets. I would set up wagers with the local thugs, betting Joey could hold his breath longer than they could, and he always won. Or bet he could beat some guy in a foot race. Who wouldn't think they could outrun a fat, thick-lipped guy wearing coke-bottle glasses? But word got around fast, so our bets dwindled to nothing. He quickly scribbled down a list of things he needed to make our final push and sent me out on the street to collect them. One of the items was a hospital bed.

It took me a few days to "find" all the stuff, but when it was finally assembled, Joey's bedroom looked like a cubicle in an ER ward—a hospital bed, IV stand, heart monitor, and a bucket that Joey had positioned on the floor at the head of the bed. I'd even found a cute little blue johnny for him. I tried not to look at his brown scaly butt when he'd turn around.

"So, what's next?" I asked. He handed me a piece of paper with an official-looking raised seal at the bottom. "What's this?"

"It's a signed and notarized statement of the terms of my death, and you're going to kill me, though not really," he said as he lay down on the hospital bed, his head hanging over the edge.

I started to back out of the room. "I'm a lot of things, but I'm not a killer."

"Of course, you're not ... friend," Joey said.

I stopped, as always. We only had each other.

"Please don't leave. Let me explain," he said, turning his big blue magnified eyes toward me. "First, you're going to hook up the

145

two IVs. Then," he said, reaching under the sheet and withdrawing a samurai sword, "you're going to decapitate me." He held up the gleaming sword. Sunlight sparkled invitingly off its shining steel.

"That would be considered murder, don't you think?" I said, snatching the sword out of his hands.

"Not the way I've set it up," he said. "As we know, cockroaches can live without their head but will die of thirst after a week. And with their head, they can live for a month without food. I've solved this problem with the IVs. One will provide me with fluids, the other

with nutrition, so I will live indefinitely in the Shrine of Roach Supreme that you will build with the billions we're gonna make. Providing that you continue to feed me."

"But then you won't—"

"Yes, I know, I'm making the ultimate sacrifice, but it's worth it if I can save humanity from certain destruction. With all the great powers of the world endowed with the serum, there will be no point in setting off a nuclear blast. I will be happy to exist in my headless, vegetative state, knowing that all is right with the world and I'm rich."

"How will you know? You won't have a brain."

He waved me off. "Don't bore me with trivialities. After you've lopped off my head, I want you to go to the cops and tell them you've discovered a grisly murder. This will bring in the media. At this point, you reveal our plan using my signed and notarized affidavit as evidence and start reaping the benefits. Just make sure you dress me in a white silk gown with gold brocade."

"Something's bound to go wrong," I said.

"Think, my friend! Think!" he exhorted.

How could I think? I sank to my knees and cried.

He patted me on the head. "There, there, little guy. Listen carefully. I'm only going to say this once. How can you be accused of murder if I'm still alive?"

I gazed at him through tear-stained eyes. I could have sworn his head was rimmed with a golden halo. I stood up, positioned myself at his head, and raised the sword toward the heavens. Giving him a loving smile, I swung the sword down with all my might. The one good deed I had ever managed. Then dialed 911. As the phone rang, I watched curiously as Joey's blood spurted out of his severed neck.

Things didn't quite work out the way we had imagined. Joey's plan had one fatal flaw, and I was too stupid to pick up on it.

The cops arrived first, guns drawn, and then the medics pronounced Joey dead at the scene. Media type crushed in at the door, cameras rolling. I was in my element.

"He's not dead," I said with a snicker.

The cops didn't think that was very funny and ordered me to the floor.

"Wait a minute," I said calmly and held out Joey's signed and notarized affidavit.

The sergeant in charge read it. "So, you did this?"

I nodded with pride.

The sergeant got in my face. "If he's still alive, how come the heart monitor ain't beepin'?" he growled.

A murmur went up among the growing crowd of onlookers.

A little confused, I looked over at the silent heart monitor. "Good question," I said. "Maybe it's not plugged in?" I made a move toward the monitor, but two other cops grabbed me, threw me down on my stomach, and handcuffed me.

The sergeant stepped on my back, grabbed my hair, and yanked my head up so that I was staring into his eyes—upside down.

"Do you know what happens when you cut off someone's head?" the sergeant said.

I wanted to say, "No, because I've never done it before," but I just gurgled.

"They bleed to death, you moron," the sergeant hissed, then smashed my head on the floor. I got a bloody nose from that one.

So, here I sit on death row. I curse Joey from time to time, but hey, you can't blame the guy. He did invent a serum that could save humanity from certain destruction—just not me.

MAUDE & LYMAN GO TO THE AIRPORT

My wife Maude wasn't superstitious, but when we woke up at dawn on this particular Sunday, she was in a state. Before her eyes opened, she said, "I had two nightmares and didn't sleep a wink."

I pointed out the obvious, but she wasn't going to have any of that.

"You know me, Lyman. I never have nightmares. It was terrible."

It was always best to humor Maude when she had her mind set. "Maybe if you tell me about it, you'll feel better."

She rambled on about being at the airport and asking our daughter Jody to watch the new kitten and the bags while she went to the ticket counter and coming back to find them gone and seeing our little terrier Rudy walk up with the kitten's head in his mouth, biting down and dropping the kitten on the cold tile with its brains spilling out.

I suggested a strong cup of tea would get her mind off such things and dragged myself out of bed. When Maude doesn't sleep, I don't either.

"And wouldn't you know it's raining and windy," she said.

"Your point, dear?"

"I shouldn't get on the plane."

"I checked the weather last night, and it's going to be a perfect day to fly."

Just as I predicted, Maude had a brighter outlook after I'd brought her a steaming cup of caffeine. She bustled about getting the house in shape for her month's absence. She and Jody were going

149

out west to care for Maude's ailing sister, and I was to stay home with Rudy, who happened to be deaf, blind, and incontinent, and Tizzy, our epileptic cat with a bladder infection. Both needed their daily meds. "Three peas in a pod," she was fond of saying. She was taking the kitten.

"I would just die if anything happened to her," she said when I told her I was perfectly capable of feeding another cat.

I had reminded both of them that we needed to leave at ten-thirty sharp to make it to the airport in time. Jody unexpectedly took off at nine to meet a friend in town to get her favorite sweatshirt she'd forgotten after a sleepover. She just had to have it for the trip. Forty-five minutes later, her friend called and asked where Jody was. Maude panicked.

"Lyman, I just know something has happened," she said, backing toward the laundry room with an armful of my dirty clothes.

I'd told her not to bother, that I could do my own laundry, but she insisted, saying that I didn't know dirty laundry from dirty dishes. The laundry room also contained cat litter and food. We'd recently put up a baby gate—Rudy liked going in there to mark his territory.

"She's had an accident or was picked up for speeding," Maude said.

"Maude, you'd better watch—"

Maude tripped over the baby gate and went down like a sack of potatoes. Fortunately, she'd added some ample padding over the years.

"Don't think I broke anything."

She's a tough old bird, is all I can say.

Jody waltzed in at ten-fifteen. Seems she and her friend had their meeting place confused, but she got the sweatshirt in the end.

Jody and I were in the car, all packed and waiting for Maude. And waiting. I went back into the house and found her on the floor in the guest room, trying to coax the kitty out from under the bed.

"It's getting late," I said.

"Don't you think I know that, Lyman?" With that, she lunged and came out with the kitty by the scruff of its neck. Poor thing looked dazed.

By now, we were late. Not more than five minutes from our house, we crested Howe Hill at a pretty good clip. I knew the road like the back of my bald head, and there wasn't another car in sight. It was still raining, but other than that, the road conditions were perfect.

"Cop!" Maude yelled.

By the time I was able to process the information and put on the brakes, the squad car lights were flashing. I grimaced and pulled over in front of it.

"Now be nice, Lyman. You remember last time? When the officer asked you why you were going so fast, and you said, 'Just cruising'?"

I grunted and opened the window just as the officer appeared. He was a pleasant-looking man. Guessed him to be about my age. Could tell by the heavy eyelids and droopy jowls. When he asked for my license, I reached for the glove compartment.

"Your wallet, dear," Maude said, smiling at the officer. "We're trying to get to the airport, and we're a little behind schedule."

The officer smiled back.

Don't they ask for your registration first? I thought as I dug out my wallet.

The officer was extremely polite and even suggested that I could make payments on the hundred and fifty dollars fine if I found it a hardship. Coupled with the three hundred dollar fine I got in the work zone a month ago, it looked like my only option.

I was steaming when we headed on our way. "Don't they have anything better to do than pick up law-abiding citizens on a desolate road?"

Maude patted my hand. "They have to make their quota, dear."

"Quota, shmota. What do I have now? Six points in the last month? Our insurance is going to go through the roof." I laid on the horn for punctuation.

"Calm down, dear. You heard the officer. If you go for two years without an infraction, the points go away."

We were low on gas. That took a few more minutes of our precious time, not to mention the outlandish fuel prices gouging my credit card.

I zoomed up the ramp and onto the interstate, not in much of a "yielding" mood.

"What I want to know is how do these gas stations get away with raising the price daily of gas they bought a month ago? It's not like it's costing them anymore just sitting there."

"It's complicated," Maude said. "You should watch the news more."

I accelerated. "A hundred and fifty bucks out the window."

"Slow down, Lyman. You just got stopped, remember?" Maude said.

My urge was to get it over with and speed down the highway until no more points were left in my bank. "They want my license? They can have it!"

I looked in the rear-view mirror to check for flashing lights. Jody smiled back at me.

"Breathe, Dad. It's in the past. Nothing you can do about it."

By Jiminy, maybe all that college tuition was paying off. I grumbled and set the car on cruise control.

We made it to the airport but were late. And then there was the kitten. Maude had drugged her on the way up and was going to try and sneak her on the plane without paying the extra hundred bucks for a "pet" ticket. A ticket for a kitten you could fit in the palm of your hand. Don't get me started.

Maude's bag was overweight by three pounds. An extra twenty-five bucks. I remember when you got a five-course meal with real silverware included in the ticket price.

I watched from the other side of the glass as Maude, the comatose kitten, and Jody made it through security without having to suffer more than removing shoes, a spread-the-legs body scan, a bomb search, and a few over-sized cosmetic containers being tossed into the garbage.

I waved goodbye and headed for home, on cruise control.

I reached our town and stopped at the post office. When I came out, I noticed a river of yellow paint running past me and down the road. I followed the river back up and saw yellow streaks and splotches all over the passenger side of my car. Somewhere along the trip, I'd run over freshly painted road lines. The rain must have helped to spread them.

I spent half an hour in the rain with the hose, Goo-Be-Gone, and a sponge, getting most of the paint off before it dried on, what the dealer called, my "silver avocado" car. I called it gray.

I stepped through our front door and slipped on a giant hairball. Rudy barked at the wall.

Ready to put this trying day behind me, I collapsed on the couch and turned on the tube, looking forward to a Red Sox game. They had the day off. Wouldn't you know?

THESE THINGS HAPPEN

We'd lost our power during the night. I was staring out the window, bemoaning the fact that I couldn't watch the morning news when my wife of forty years came in.

"Would you stop looking at that barn, Lyman? It's driving me crazy," Maude said.

"That barn ain't worth looking at," I said.

Maude patted my shoulder. "I know it's ruined your view, but there's nothing we can do about it now."

"A view I had for twenty-five years," I said. "He could have put it across the road. Wouldn't have bothered anyone."

"When you have that kind of money, I guess you can build a barn wherever you please," she said. "Just forget about it."

"And I suppose you don't care about all the trees he cut down on the property line. He can see right into our bathroom."

Maude laughed. "That's why I put up the curtains."

"Well, I don't live in the country to put up curtains."

"Mr. Grumpy Pants needs his coffee."

After coffee, I put on my boots and overalls and went out to assess the damage. Been freezing rain all night on top of the two feet of snow, so most of the trees were bent over like sometimes I feel in the morning, their branches weighed down with a half inch of ice. Some damn tree on the line must have caused the outage. Had to admit, with the morning sun glinting off the ice and snow, looked like some kind of wonderland. The driveway was blocked with hanging boughs, not that I planned to go anywhere, but you never know. When you're old, you can have a heart attack or something at any time.

I grabbed my pruning shears out of the shed. That's when I heard a loud *crack* coming from the woods back of the house. A few seconds later, an even louder *crash*. Made me jump.

There goes a birch, I thought. First to go in a storm like this. Can't take the strain. Hell, all the trees were in trouble.

I headed down the driveway, shaking drooping limbs to try and free 'em from the ice. When that didn't work, I cut 'em back till they rose up enough to let a car pass. I was about to the end of the driveway when I heard another loud *crack*. I looked up and watched a tall poplar come crashing down on the other side of the road. It hit the power line stretched over my driveway, and the crackling wire whipped through the air. Had to dive out of the way so it didn't kill me. Scraped my cheek on the ice (at least I didn't break a hip).

I'd called the electric company's automated power outage service first thing in the morning but was pleased that now I could call back and "press three to report flickering lights or lines down on the road." But it didn't matter because our phone was dead. I thought maybe Mr. Money up the road would call it in. I was pretty sure he had one of them newfangled cell phones.

Late next morning Maude and I were huddled around the gas kitchen stove, our only source of heat, wondering if maybe we shouldn't go somewhere nicer. I suggested Florida, but Maude, ever practical, thought maybe our daughter's down to Concord.

We debated the finer points of "gypsy coffee" (when you throw the old grinds back into a pot along with eggshells and whatnot and keep it on simmer) when I heard a vehicle rumbling up the road. It was the pretty white and orange of the electric company, and it stopped right at the bottom of our driveway.

I ambled down. Didn't want to appear too anxious among these heroes of the community. There were two of them in full gear, with orange hardhats, sunglasses, orange overalls, and big boots. Laden tool belts hung from their fit waists. In spite of the cold, they didn't wear gloves. They sure looked efficient.

"What's the damage?" I asked.

"About three thousand customers out," the bigger one said as he untangled the live wire.

"Lucky you have a downed line blocking your driveway," said the smaller, putting on some kind of climbing harness. "Top priority. Some folks could be out for weeks."

"Hey there, fellas," came a voice from up the road.

Mr. Money, coffee mug in hand, swaggered toward us. "Knew it was hot," he said. "Bet you thought it was the phone line, Lyman. Most people do."

"The phone died when it went down," I said.

"I know these things. I'm a volunteer fireman. You should join up, Lyman. Or maybe you're too old?" Mr. Money laughed.

The two workers weren't paying much attention to Mr. Money and me. They just kept working. Mr. Money stepped in front of the big one un-kinking the downed line.

"You know, if you fellas cut down that row of poplars, we wouldn't have this problem again," Mr. Money said.

The Big One brushed past him as he strung the line on the ground between the two poles.

"Can you make it happen?" Mr. Money asked.

Big One stopped and studied Money through his sunglasses. "You hunt?"

Mr. Money shuffled his feet. "Some. Not much, but I like hunters. I have guns."

"This your land?" Big One asked with a sweeping gesture.

Mr. Money smiled. "About two hundred acres worth. Own both sides of the road up to the ridges, except for Lyman's patch here. Own everything up back of him, though."

"Looks posted," Big One said.

"One time, I found some guy taking aim at my house from the road, right from his truck," I piped up.

"You let anyone hunt your land?" Big One asked Mr. Money.

Mr. Money took a slug of coffee and looked Big One up and down. "Let me see what you look like. Take off your glasses."

Big One hesitated but then took them off.

Mr. Money leaned in. "Okay. How about your hard hat?"

Who does Money think he is, I wondered, asking some man he hasn't even met properly to take off personal pieces of clothing in the middle of a dead-end dirt road?

Big One cocked his head but then shrugged, tilted his head forward, and the hardhat dropped into his hand. The sun reflected off his bald head.

"All right," Mr. Money said, tipping back his own woolen cap and showing off his bald head. "We're brothers in that department." He gave Big One another going over. "Come hunt any time."

Big One put his hard hat back on. "Thanks. Probably be up this afternoon."

"When do you think we'll get power back?" I asked.

"About two hours," Small One said as he shimmied up the pole, line in hand.

I clapped my mittens. "Great. Good work. Thank you."

"Let's have a cigar," Mr. Money said, passing them around.

I took one and tucked it into my overalls.

Mr. Money lit up and blew out a smoke ring. "So how about those poplars?" he said to Big One.

"Not our job. Gotta call the town."

That afternoon Maude and I were watching a rerun of Jeopardy when I heard a rifle shot in the woods up back the house.

"What the bejesus?" I peered out the window. "I knew this would happen. That damn Money. There ain't been any hunters up there for twenty years."

Maude patted my knee. "Don't worry, Lyman. Hunters don't usually mistake a house for deer."

Another shot exploded outside, and the window behind Maude shattered inward, glass flying everywhere. She screamed and fell to

159

the floor, her head missing the coffee table's sharp edge. She grabbed her neck. I dove on top of her to shield her from more danger.

"Maude, you all right?" I yelled.

"I think I'll live," Maude said. "If you get off me."

I sat up, straddling her, gently pulling her hand off her neck. There was a red welt a couple of inches long just below her ear.

"Just grazed you," I said, rolling off her.

"I was born lucky." Maude sat up and gingerly felt the wound. "I'll get some ice."

I looked out the broken window and saw a flash of orange disappearing into a pine grove. "I'll get some plastic."

I stormed up the road toward Money's house. His big black 4X4 pulled out of the driveway and headed toward me. I waved him down, and he lowered his window. I could see his good-looking wife in the passenger seat.

"Nice getting the power back, eh, Lyman?" Money said.

"That damn power guy shot my wife," I said, my tone louder than I'd intended.

"My god," said Money's wife.

"I'll call 911. Got my radio right here," Money said, reaching for it.

"She's okay. Just a flesh wound. But I tell you, Money, you were wrong letting that guy hunt up behind my house," I said.

"Well, hell, Lyman, it's my land, and you know, that's New England for you. These things happen."

How would he know 'That's New England'? Flatlander only lived here three years.

"Like I said, those poplars were down, wouldn't have had this problem in the first place. I'll do it tomorrow," Money said.

"I'll give you a hand," I said.

Money laughed. "Doing what, old man? Watching?"

I glared at him.

"Just having some fun, Lyman. Lighten up. Hey, we're going to town, have a nice dinner at the Inn. You have a good night." He revved the truck.

I could see his wife nudging him. He turned to her, and she mumbled something. He turned back.

"Oh yeah, sorry about Marge."

"Maude."

"I was close!"

With that, Money gunned the truck and took off down the road. Sprayed some gravel on me.

It was near dark when I fired up the chainsaw. I had at those trees like they were the last thing standing between me and a strong cup of coffee. Maude didn't think it was a good idea, but I told her Money was going to do it tomorrow anyway, and besides, it was the neighborly thing to do. Helping out, and all. She didn't disagree with that, being the kind soul she is.

It didn't take long to fell them dozen poplars—skinny things far as trees go. Crashed straight down the road like a row of dead drunks. Have to buck 'em up some time to clear the way, but thought that could wait. Had more important things to do. Besides, Money was the only one who lived above us and wouldn't be home for a few hours. If I didn't have 'em cleared by then, he and his wife only have to walk a hundred yards to their house. No matter. As Money kept pointing out, they were young yet.

The full moon cast a pleasant glow on the barn. Money had spared no expense (he'd made sure to let me know that), and I had to admit, it was pretty good-looking, natural siding and all. I pulled back the heavy sliding door and stepped in. The smell of dry hay made my nostrils twitch.

I climbed up to the loft and sat down on a comfortable bale at the base of the big stack. Kicked open the top bay and looked out across the countryside. The moonlight on all that snow and ice made everything sparkle.

I leaned back and pulled the cigar from my overalls. Gave it a sniff and bit off the end, like I seen 'em do in the gangster movies. Struck a match and sucked hard. Filled my mouth with smoke and swirled it around. Tasted pretty good till I remembered I didn't smoke and tossed the cigar over my shoulder.

I lounged on the sofa, looking out the picture window. Took a sip of hot chocolate my good wife had brought me. She sat next to me with an icepack on her neck, her nose buried in her knitting. A rerun of Jeopardy was on TV.

"Looking at that barn again, Lyman?" she asked.

"Just enjoying the view," I said.

"You haven't enjoyed that view in two years," she said.

"Seems to get better with age."

162

Maude looked up from her knitting and stared out the window. "They have a woodstove in that barn?"

"Must," I said.

She studied the curl of smoke rising from the top of the barn. "I think I see flames shooting out the hayloft."

"Could be moonlight," I said.

She stood up and pressed her nose up against the window. "Those are flames, Lyman. The barn's on fire!"

"Let me get a closer look. Eyes ain't what they used to be." I stood beside her at the window.

She pointed down the road. "Here come some lights."

I could see the headlights of Money's 4X4 speeding up the road. He always drove too fast for my liking. The truck skidded to a stop just before hitting the row of downed poplars.

Looking over to the barn, I could see it was now fully engaged, flames licking out every way. I saw Money jump down from his truck and run up the road. He kept tripping over the poplars, falling down, and getting up. I could hear his curses.

"We better call 911, Lyman," Maude said.

"Money can handle it. He's a volunteer fireman."

I sat back down on the couch, took a sip of hot chocolate, and settled in to watch the rest of the show.

TORTOISE

I'm not sure how old I am. I know a tortoise can live a long time. I'm told Grandfather Tort lived to be two hundred and twenty. My father Ort and mother Toisé are still alive and must be at least two hundred. Making me, Ort Junior, maybe a hundred and eighty. You can see how it might be a problem keeping exact track of the years.

You've probably surmised by how we move that we also think very slowly—counting to ten is not an easy task. The time between thoughts is vast, and for the uninitiated (we call them the "un-tortled"), it doesn't take much to lose track. Try counting ten breaths, just the inhales.

I'm assuming that you are human if you are reading this and, thus, can be easily distracted. Even those of you who think you are "enlightened." You can cruise along for minutes, days, maybe years with complete focus and concentration, but something will trip you up in the end. The standing joke with us is, "What's the difference between a human and a tortoise?" Hmm, not as easy as you thought it might be? Coming from a turtle? Don't worry. We've had eons to ponder the answer. I'll give you some more time.

What I'm driving at is that true equanimity—or "Slow Mind," as our elders put it—is easier to achieve for a tortoise than a human. In spite of your so-called "patience," you are unable to truly stand still in body or mind. Now don't get angry. In fact, anger is another one of your problems. I hate to say this, but your general makeup is not made for success, or, should I say, success doesn't come easily for you. We have an old saying—if you want something done right, don't ask a human (sorry).

My children, of whom I have a countless number (countless because I'm still counting them), and I have a standing joke when we're out driving. They shout, "Here comes our exit! Turn!" And I shout back, "I'm trying!" Then we zoom past it and laugh. Whenever we get on the Interstate, it's an adventure because we can never get off. Unlike you humans who, it seems, must always have a destination, we drive till we come to the end of the road and see what's there. And we're never in a hurry to go home, mainly because we'd never get there.

The one you called the Buddha was on the right track. I understand that he was able to sit still for long periods of time and made some remarkable discoveries pertaining to peace of mind and how to alleviate suffering. We applaud him and hope that there are others out there like him. But if you want a meditation lesson, come to my house. I've been sitting in the same place for years and never had one thought cross my mind, let alone a disturbing one.

You might think my thinking is scattered, jumping from one subject to the next, but you forget that my ideas have been germinating for a long time, some for decades, before I allow them to be expressed. This is how you avoid conflict, which seems to be your main problem. Why can't you get along with your neighbor? Why do you shout back and forth until it eventually comes to blows? Take it from me, a tortoise, that there is nothing to get upset about. For me, us, by the time we've formed an opinion about something, whatever it was about has long since disappeared. Like a juicy grasshopper perched on a blade of grass—in the time it takes to open our mouths to chomp, it's gone.

We really do appreciate being immortalized in your wonderful fable, "The Tortoise & The Hare." You had it right that being slow and steady is one of the primary rules of success. But you humans have an annoying trait. I don't mean to be picky or mean-spirited, but it's like this: you get a good idea, run with it for a while, then forget about it and go about your agonizing ways. You don't seem to be able to maintain any mental stability. What is it your Buddha said? About the mind being so swiftly moving, seizing whatever it

165

wants? He had that right. You'll go along fine for a while with a clear mind and pure intentions, and then, SNAP! Something happens, and you go haywire. It's sad. We've watched many kingdoms and cultures come and go. Species, too. Humanoid and otherwise. And I'm afraid yours is no different. Only because, even though you know the "secret," you fail to use it, at least for any length of time. I guess "suffers from short attention span" is the simplest way to put it. If you only realized that it takes common sense and perseverance to prevail. It's frustrating. You have everything it takes to become enlightened, and I'm not talking nickels and dimes. I'm talking about the entire population of the planet.

I guess it boils down to humility. You just don't have it. You "think, therefore you are" is not a philosophy to base your actions upon. This is obvious, isn't it? All you've been able to accomplish over thousands, millions of years, is to become more and more unconscious and violent, leading you on an inexorable path to self-annihilation. Please wake up. It's "you are, therefore you think"— isn't it obvious that you first appear as an aware being before any thought is formed? And thinking, as we've discovered (tortoises, that is) only leads to trouble. Fortunately for us, there is such a distance between thoughts that we've never been able to act on them. Our actions are based on pure knowledge, knowledge in the absence of thought.

Ask yourself, "Do I ever act compulsively? Some of you, trying to be good parents, teach your children to "think before you act". But now we are getting into a realm that is beyond you. I'm sure you're getting confused, because haven't I said that right action does not involve "thinking"? You're probably thinking at this moment, "This tortoise doesn't know what he's talking about." But I do. What has been lost in translation over the years is that this was originally stated as "pause before you act." In the silence between thoughts, right action will arise.

You're probably saying to yourself, "How can this pompous pontificating terrapin speak of humility?" Because we "do" very little. And we are *not* swamp dwellers, as you infer. When you are content to live a simple life without trying to "make things better," especially when it involves imposing your "good" ideas on someone else, then clarity becomes the norm. Then you can speak, if you must, the Truth. And, as you say but don't do, "the truth will set you free." I do get a kick out of your quaint sayings.

You might think I'm rambling, but for me, that's impossible. As I've mentioned, or not, a "thought" for me is a precious thing— not something I take lightly, as you humans are prone to do. I've known you to have tens of thousands of thoughts in one day. I'm lucky if I have one thought in a thousand days. So, I pay attention. I scan the vast emptiness of my mind like a hawk hovering over a vast meadow in search of a juicy rodent. And when one comes into view, I dive. But do I then kill and devour? No. I embrace the lonely little thought in the soft tissue between my carapace and plastron (for you, the heart). I coo and caress. I know that this sweet little thought has but a short life, and I must tend to it with loving care as it dissolves back into nothingness. That's how you do it.

You're probably asking yourself how, with my insistence that a tortoise only has one thought in many days or years, can I ramble on like a madman? It's true that we have very few thoughts, but the ones we do have, we never forget. We store them up for a rainy day (isn't that one of your favorite expressions?). It's one of a tortoise's favorite past times—to talk. And to be able to talk, you must have a string of consecutive thoughts, which, for us, takes years to accumulate. But once we have them, watch out. Conversations can go on for quite some time. You wouldn't believe how long it took me to get this little discourse you're reading down on paper.

I'd love to keep up this dialogue with you, but I have a family reunion in Biloxi in thirty years and, being in Charlottesville for a bluegrass festival, I'd better get on my way.

In closing, I truly "think" (ha!) that you know what right action is, but you don't seem to have the gumption to follow through. It's not that we don't have our vices. We are the epitome of wisdom and have the highest moral standards, but we love to eat copious amounts of vegetation. And gamble ... on you, as in, what and when will you do something stupid? A lot of lettuce greens (our favorite) are won and lost on these questions, though the "when?" is more challenging. We know you will do something stupid even if you've been making intelligent choices for a while. Cruising along, doing fine, then—BOOM! You lose it. Always. How can we be so sure? We have spent countless hours observing. Remember, to sit immobile is our forte. When you watch human activity with detachment, it doesn't take long to recognize a habit pattern— sooner or later, KAPLOOEY!

And that riddle I posed earlier? The difference between a tortoise and a human? Hard one, I know, and I promise to tell you the answer. But it might take a while.

TIME FLIES

Bob slugged another shot of tequila and slammed down the empty glass on the bar. "I wish he would die," he said to no one in particular. The few remaining clientele paid him no mind. Bob was a regular, and they'd heard it all before.

A finely dressed gentleman ambled up to the bar and sat down on a stool next to Bob, who wobbled a bit on his but then caught his balance. The gentleman raised a finger, and the bartender came over.

"Two more of the same," the gentleman said in a rich baritone with an indiscernible accent, pointing to Bob's empty shot glass. "And bring the bottle." The bartender nodded, reached behind him, and filled the order.

The gentleman passed a full glass to Bob. "I would be honored to share a drink with you."

Bob stared at the gentleman through his drunken haze, then picked up the fresh shot and downed it. "Thanks," Bob said. The gentlemen took a leisurely drink, set his shot glass on the counter, and refreshed the empties.

"You're my kind of man," Bob said, fingering the filled glass as he stared at his disheveled image in the mirror behind the bar.

"I happened to hear what you said a while ago, and if you don't mind me asking, do you wish someone dead?" the gentleman asked.

"My father," Bob answered sullenly.

"I can help you," the gentleman said.

Bob spun around on his stool too quickly, making a complete rotation before the gentleman put out a hand and stopped his progress. "I'm not looking to hire anyone," and then with lowered voice through clenched teeth, "to kill my father."

The gentleman burst out laughing. "I would hope not. Please tell me what you meant then. If you don't mind."

"Hell no, I don't mind. Everyone in this place knows my story," Bob said. "To put it simply, my father's a self-made man worth about twenty million bucks that I'll inherit when he dies. The only problem is that could take another forty years, and by that time, I'll be too old to enjoy the money."

"How old are you?" the gentleman asked.

"Thirty-eight."

"And your father?"

"Sixty and he swears he'll live to be a hundred."

"But at, hmm, seventy-eight, surely you could enjoy the money."

"Ha. Right. Buy a lifetime supply of diapers."

"But surely you must have a life worth living right now."

"I have no life. I have no ambition. I'm a spoiled rich kid who works for his father. For peanuts, I might add. He owns me."

"I can see your dilemma," the gentleman said, taking another sip of tequila. "What if I told you that your father was going to die of a heart attack at seventy?"

"I'd kiss your ass," Bob said, downing his shot.

The gentleman chuckled. "You don't have to do that, but you never know how long anyone is going to live. It's all quite random, don't you think?"

"I try not to," Bob said as the gentleman refilled his glass.

"I can speed up time for you if that would be of any help," the gentleman said, wiping his lips with a napkin. "It would ensure, if my guess is right, that you would inherit the money with plenty of time left to enjoy it."

Bob puts down his full glass and looks at the gentleman. "Sounds perfect, but I wasn't born yesterday, mister. What's the catch?"

"I would call it a business proposition."

"And?"

"When your father dies, I get half the money."

"That's it?'

"That's it."

Bob reached out his hand, and the two shook on the deal. "Where should I send the check?"

The gentleman laughed. "I wasn't born yesterday, either. Meet me back here when your father dies."

"How will you know?" Bob asked.

The gentleman smiled at him. "I'll read it in the paper?"

Bob staggered off but stopped and turned back. "Wait a minute. How do I know if you can actually speed up time?"

"You'll just have to trust me. If it doesn't happen, the deal is null and void."

Bob nodded his head, satisfied with the answer. "Ok. What should I do in the meantime? Ten years is a long time."

The gentleman gave Bob a sly little grin. "Just continue to live your meaningless life. Pay little attention to anything, and it will go fast enough."

"That'll be easy," Bob said.

Ten years passed, and for Bob, in his oblivious haze, it went by in a blink of an eye. Almost to the day, his father died of a heart attack, and Bob inherited the family fortune, now valued at thirty million. A week later, Bob, somewhat reluctantly, went back to the bar with a check for ten million dollars. The gentleman sat at the bar sipping a shot of tequila. A full shot glass awaited Bob as he sat down next to him.

"Sorry I'm late," Bob said. "A lot to deal with in the past week."

The gentleman raised his glass. "No problem. Cheers."

Bob looked at the shot and passed. "Quit drinking a week ago. I'm engaged."

The gentleman nodded his head approvingly. "Going to make something of your life after all?"

"Now that I have the money, it's about time, speaking of which," and Bob handed an envelope to the gentleman. Bob tensed slightly and held his breath as the gentleman opened it and peeked at the check inside.

The gentleman smiled at Bob. "Very good."

Bob, relieved, exhaled as he stood up. "See you around, then?"

"Our business is done, so I doubt it," the gentleman said, reaching into his breast pocket. "But, if by chance you ever need me." He handed Bob a business card.

Bob snickered. "That's rare. As if I need anybody now." He turned and walked out of the pub.

Bob settled into his role as head of his father's business empire. He soon married his fiancé, and nine months later, they had a beautiful baby girl. Bob's life was now perfect. He had a family to live for and, for the first time in his life, ambition—to not only succeed in business to add to his already huge fortune, now valued at fifty million dollars—but to become a better person for his wife and child.

One day, not too long after his daughter's birth, he came home from the office and was greeted at the front door by a girl who, by looking at her size, must have been about ten years old.

"Hello, Daddy," the girl said.

Bob gave the girl a confused look.

"Do you like my new dress?" the girl asked.

"Amy?"

"Oh, Daddy, you're so funny," Amy said and gave her father a hug. "Come, Mommy has dinner waiting for you." And she led him off.

Later that night, Bob and his wife were getting ready for bed.

"Amy is really growing up fast, don't you think?" Bob said to his wife.

"She's growing up like any other normal child," his wife said.

Bob shook his head. "I don't know. It seems like only yesterday she was still in diapers."

"Maybe you're too busy making money to notice the changes. It's all right. That's what men do," his wife said.

The next day Bob, held late at the office for a meeting, came home early evening and saw a strange car in the driveway. He walked up to his front entrance and reached for the doorknob. The door burst open. Out rushed a beautiful teenage girl with a handsome teenage boy. Bob put his hand out to make them stop before they knocked him over.

"Wait a minute, who are you?" Bob said with some desperation.

The girl turned to the boy. "He thinks he's a comedian." Then to Bob. "Sorry, Daddy, but we're late for the prom." She grabbed the boy's hand and started to move past Bob.

"Amy? What's going on? Who's this boy?" Bob demanded.

Amy looked at her father as though he was crazy. "Chad, my steady boyfriend of three years? You better go take a nap." She giggled, and the teenagers rushed off.

Bob went into the foyer and stared at himself in the large hall mirror. At that moment, his wife came in.

"Hi, dear, let me take your coat," she said.

Without taking his eyes off his reflection in the mirror, he said, "When did my hair turn gray?"

His wife laughed. "You are a funny man and also quite young looking for your age. At least that's what my girlfriends tell me."

"How old am I?" Bob asked.

His wife looked at him, puzzled. "Seriously?"

"Please?"

"Well, dear, last I knew, you were sixty-six," she said, crossing her arms. "Maybe you should go see the doctor."

Bob ran past her and up the stairs to his bedroom. He frantically searched his closet and came out holding a business card.

Bob charged into his old pub. His eyes were immediately drawn to the bar, where the finely dressed gentleman sat calmly pouring tequila into two shot glasses. Bob marched over.

"What's going on?" Bob said, and not with a friendly tone.

The gentleman smiled and handed Bob a drink. Bob downed it in one gulp and clutched the empty glass.

"I thought you quit drinking," the gentleman said.

"I've changed," Bob said.

The gentleman looked Bob up and down. "Change is the one certainty we can rely upon."

Bob slammed his shot glass on the bar. "Cut the crap, Mr. Know-it-All. You've done something to my family and me. I've aged twenty years in the last two days."

"Very perceptive," the gentleman said. "As the old saying goes, time flies when you're having a good time."

"I haven't been able to enjoy any of my life since you came into it. One day my daughter was born, I turned around, and I'd missed her entire childhood. I want it to stop," Bob said with escalating volume.

The bartender came over, ready to diffuse any confrontation. Bob waved him off.

"Why are you doing this to me?" Bob asked the gentleman.

"Why do you think?" the gentlemen asked.

"I don't have to think. I gave you ten million dollars," Bob shouted.

At this, the pub chatter halted. Some clientele paused mid-drink.

"Yes, but that wasn't half now, was it?" the gentleman responded in a quiet voice.

Bob leaned in. "More money? Is that what you want? Ok, fine." He reached into his breast pocket and pulled out a checkbook, furiously scribbled on it, and handed it to the gentleman, who looked at it.

"Five million dollars?" the gentleman said with disdain.

"That's it. That's the rest of your half of the thirty million," Bob said with finality.

The gentleman burst out with laughter that went on for some time. When he finally stopped, he said, "As you would say, that's rare."

Bob got right in the gentleman's face. Very deliberately, he said, "What do you want to stop this madness?"

The gentleman took a sip of his tequila, then dabbed his lips with a napkin. "It would insult your limited intelligence to have to articulate my demands. That being said, I think you know the answer as well as I do."

COFFEE AT THE MIDNIGHT DINER

Night. Cold drizzle. A naked man walks backward. Disheveled hair hangs in his face. He drags something heavy. Pulling, straining, his back bends with the effort. He lurches ahead a foot at a time. His eyes dart, peer into storefronts and shadowed alcoves, unto the street at the occasional passing car. The drizzle turns to steady rain.

He slips on the slick pavement. Regains his balance. Stops to catch his breath. Brushes hair, wet with rain and sweat, from his brow. His eyes show a feral desperation, a beast in flight.

A couple, arm in arm, walks toward him. He presses up against a brick wall and pulls whatever he's dragging along with him. Holds his breath. The couple looks him up and down. He watches them pass and exhales. He looks down. He holds a hand attached to a pale bare arm, leading to a bruised and naked body. He stares into the vacant eyes of a woman with long black hair.

He grabs the woman's other hand. With this two-fisted grip, he drags the cumbersome body down the sidewalk. Foot traffic increases as he nears an intersection, but no one seems to notice the naked man dragging a body.

He waits for the light to change. Starts off across the street backward, dragging the body. He reaches the middle of the intersection. A squad car, lights flashing, siren blaring, bears down on him. He freezes. It speeds on past. He sucks in a lungful of air. Lugs the body through the intersection, trips on the curb, and collapses on the sidewalk. Have to find some clothes, he thinks. Dragging his load with one hand, he crawls until he reaches the safety of a comforting dark alley.

The naked man dangles from the waist, head first in a dumpster. His legs flop in the air. The woman on the ground below him. He throws garbage over his shoulder. A partially eaten pork chop lands on the woman's chest. With a grunt, he pulls up a garbage bag and drops it on the pavement. He jumps down, rips open the bag, and pours out the rotting contents. He holds up the empty bag and examines it, then looks at the body. He takes the pork chop off its chest.

The man stuffs the woman feet first into the empty garbage bag. The bag comes up to her waist, where he knots it so it won't slip off. Reaching from behind, he slips his arms under her armpits and lifts her up, but it's hard for her to stand—too tipsy with her legs in the bag. He lowers her to the ground, takes off the bag, slips it over her head, and ties it off just below her breasts. He pulls her up, puts an arm around her waist, and walks out of the alley, hauling her along at his side.

The man walks along the street, body in tow. Its legs keep getting tangled in his. He can't carry her upright without both of them looking ridiculous. He drops her. His eyes fall on the dark patch between her legs. He becomes aroused. Some passersby approach, and, embarrassed, he puts his hands over his groin. They laugh at some joke as they pass but don't look at him.

The man pulls the woman face up by her legs like he's the horse and she's the cart. He trudges along, leaning forward, straining with the weight. He looks around as though trying to get his bearings. If I could just find the apartment, he thinks.

He hears a church bell toll and stops next to a brick wall. Cloaked in darkness, he cocks an ear and counts the rings. On the stroke of twelve, a bright neon sign bursts to life on the dark wall. It spells out "Midnight Diner." He peers through a large plate glass window. With checkered tablecloths glowing in the candlelight, the interior looks warm and inviting.

He pushes the diner's door open with his head and starts in. The body gets wedged in between the closing door and the doorjamb. He pushes the door open with one hand as he pulls on the body's leg with the other. He gets the body inside before the door can close on its head. He takes a deep breath and looks around, afraid that everyone in the diner is staring at him. Even though it's crowded, no one seems to have noticed the naked man with an erection dragging a garbage bag with legs sticking out. He makes his way to the nearest empty table.

He props up the body in a chair and sits down beside it. He looks at it curiously, perhaps trying to remember who or what it is. He unties the garbage bag and slips it off. The woman slumps toward him. He catches her and holds her up. He looks into her waxen face. Her eyelids flutter. He gets a glimpse of her bloodshot eyes. She smiles and reaches down between his legs. He glances around, hoping that no one sees what she is doing. Moving slowly and sensually, she straddles him.

A waiter comes up to the naked man and woman and places two menus on their table. "Can I help you?" he asks.

The man stares at the waiter while the woman moves up and down in his lap as though she's riding a mythical creature in a rolling sea. He opens his mouth to speak but can't.

"Two coffees?" the waiter suggests.

The naked man nods and swallows hard. "One black. Cream and sugar for the lady."

TWO TO TANGO

(True Story)

"Intrigue is inevitable when a man & woman

dance, or try to dance, the tango." – Anon.

A couple of years ago, I gave my wife and myself a Christmas gift of four private ballroom dance lessons. Dana had studied ballet in her youth, and I, along with attending Saturday afternoon dance lessons as a child, had won a jitterbug contest when I was a teenager. We were ready for something like this. Besides, it was the only last-minute present I could think of.

Things didn't go quite as planned. I had a bad knee that I didn't know was bad until I started doing some "dips," and our teacher, an elegant eighty-nine-year-old diva in a leotard, accidentally tripped Dana, who fell on top of her. Physical ailments aside, it turned out that after almost thirty years of marital bliss, we weren't that compatible on the dance floor. It all boiled down to this—I was a poor leader, and Dana was a poor follower.

I did my best to keep up a cheerful front, saying how much fun I was having, but deep down, I was frustrated. Her formal dance background made it easier for her to pick up new steps, while my forte as a "twister" (do you remember Chubby Checker?) didn't translate that well to the "promenade." When the four lessons were up, so was I.

One night over dinner a year later, Dana said, "We should learn how to tango."

My fork stopped halfway to my mouth. She'd been watching too much of Dancing With The Stars. "No offense, but ..." I got the

181

look that I could freeze over hell and had to think fast. "Lessons are expensive, and ..."

She gave me a wry smile. "They're three dollars a week at the local college."

I did my best to weasel my way out, citing the gimpy knee, the always potentially bad weather, and the bad day of the week (Monday Night Football!)—I exhausted every bad thing I could think of.

When I was done with my pathetic rant, she said, still smiling, "Lessons start tomorrow."

I put on a happy face and said, "Can't wait."

We signed up for the four-week beginner's course, which was held in the basement of the college student center. If you weren't careful, you could bonk your head on the exposed heating ducts that surrounded the portable parquet dance floor. When the heat was on, the blowers drowned out the music.

Our instructor was a short, muscular Latino who moved like a panther. He lined us up like it was a military inspection. Pacing before us, he said, "I teach you tango from the streets of Buenos Aires. You learn tango, you learn your heart."

I rolled my eyes at Dana.

She gave me a look. "Pay attention."

The instructor continued. "It is a dance of love and passion."

I whispered in her ear, "I like that part."

She gave me a light slap on my hand. "Shhh!"

182

"But first, we walk," the instructor said.

He proceeded to walk us in a circle around the dance floor. Slow, fast, slow, fast. After five minutes, the girl in front of me stopped abruptly, and I bumped into her. She gave me a look. I apologized and checked my watch. Fifty minutes to go.

"Now," our instructor said, "we learn tango walk—*la Caminada*."

He took a deliberate step with his left foot, thrust his right shoulder forward, and pointed at the floor with his right forefinger. Then reversed the process, leading with his right foot. "Follow me," he said, strutting around the circle like a Furry Freak Brother.

I was sullen on the way home.

"That was pretty boring," Dana said.

I sensed a glimmer of hope. "Yeah, we already knew how to walk."

After four weeks of more walking (OMG!) and learning a basic eight-beat pattern, we graduated to the advanced beginner's class. Here we added a cool move to the pattern—*la Crusada*. Dana would take a step back with her right foot and "cross" her left foot over it.

I had to admit, I was in a mindless groove. I could lead patterns all night long and didn't have to think about a thing. It wasn't until we attended a "Special Advanced Beginner's Workshop" with a famous visiting tango instructor—a matronly woman with a thick accent (and midsection)—that I was exposed to the fraud I had become. I also got an inkling of what a baby I was.

I was feeling confident until the instructor put on the music and called out something I couldn't understand. The other participants moved gracefully, dancing in a way I was unfamiliar with. Dana noticed my anxious look.

"Don't worry about it," she said. "Let's go."

I led off with the one pattern I knew.

Like a shark smelling blood, the instructor made a beeline for us. She grabbed me by the shoulders and manipulated me every which way. "Do that," she said. "And then you dance the tango." She spun off.

I couldn't for the life of me do "that." And when men of my experience and maturity can't do something, they stop doing anything. I left a forlorn Dana standing in the middle of the floor. The instructor danced with her as I sat woodenly on the sidelines staring out a window. I was so happy to get back to my little group with the panther and do my pattern over and over.

"Many a relationship has been pushed to the limit by tango."
– Anon.

Four weeks later, we had graduated to a new time and place. We were now "Intermediates." Even I was getting tired of the same old thing, and Dana was overjoyed to go on to something new. She'd been trying to get our old instructor to teach us the *ocho*, a figure eight pattern, and each time she asked, he would say, "Next time," but it never came.

Our new instructor was a no-nonsense, enthusiastic grad student, but it soon became apparent that maybe we (as in "I") weren't true intermediates.

I couldn't pick up any new moves. In my defense, they came at me like a swarm of angry bees—*el paseo, la cadencia, la caza, la cunita.* It was a nightmare. Secretly I was worried that my brain had

184

solidified, and that I was in the early stages of dementia. After one failed attempt on my part, Dana stopped, and while moving me this way and that like she was a puppeteer, said, and I like to think, rather smugly, "Like this. It's so simple." Adrenaline rushed through my body. I froze and glared at her.

Sneaking a quick look around the room at the *advanced* dancers—no way they were beginners—I said through gritted teeth, "Not so loud."

The instructor, to her credit, noticed our dilemma and was quick to point out that Dana should resist taking over. She had a name for someone like her—*Back Leader*. She went on to explain that in the beginning, it was far more difficult to lead than it was to follow and that Dana must restrain herself. Ha! I thought. Take that.

The hours leading up to class brought out my multiple personalities. The loving husband who is willing to do anything to make his wife happy. The spoiled brat, whining that it was hopeless, asking why we were wasting our time. But nothing could dissuade Dana from "our night out."

I hated being singled out on the dance floor, especially by my own wife. For starters, I didn't like crowds, and when Dana would correct me, my face would flush, my body stiffen, and I'd refuse to dance another step. Turning my back to her gave me the greatest satisfaction. Then my other self would kick in, and I'd soften and try again.

It got so I dreaded going to lessons. It seemed that we were always being taught something new, and all I'd been able to master was the basic pattern. And it turned out that true tango was all about improvisation, that you never did it the same way twice. It appeared as though I had danced my way into Hell.

After one class that hadn't gone too well—I had repeatedly refused to try anything new and danced like a zombie—we drove home in silence. Dana finally broke the tension.

"I thought learning tango would be fun," she said.

"Right," I said, my eyes glued on the road.

"Why do you have such a bad attitude about this?" she said.

I slammed on the brakes and we sat there in the middle of the road.

Dana grimaced. "Don't be foolish."

"Foolish?" I stammered. "Foolish?"

"Please drive," Dana said. "We can talk about this when we get home."

"I don't think so," I said, putting my foot on the gas. "You're too stubborn and bossy."

We rode on in silence for a minute or two, and then Dana had to get in the last word. "You're acting like a jerk."

I tossed and turned all night. What was it about me that I couldn't take direction from Dana? Or was I unwilling to admit that I didn't understand something? Or got so embarrassed being singled out in a crowd that I acted like a child? Had I suffered some forgotten trauma in third grade at the hands of a heavy-handed dance teacher? I was a grown man who had spent most of his life trying to let go of his ego. I knew that clinging to ones limited view was a blueprint for disaster. How could you get along with anyone if you always thought you were right or, conversely, the other person was always wrong? Aarrghhh!

But I persisted. Something deep inside told me that I had to keep going. That if I valued the love that Dana and I had for each other, I'd better get it together.

Three weeks in, with many failed attempts by both Dana and our wonderful instructor to get me to comprehend, let alone learn, what was going on, the instructor mercifully suggested we go back to her beginner's class. Dana groaned. I inwardly cried out, "Yes!"

There's a happy ending to this leg of the journey. The beginner's class was perfect for me. And it turned out that I had learned some new moves along the way and was starting to improvise. Sure, I'd get stuck from time to time, but somewhere along the line Dana had developed this supreme patience and now waited until I figured things out. When I mentioned this to her, she said, "You have no idea."

ACKNOWLEDGEMENTS

I would like to extend my thanks and appreciation to my son Kevin Wright as first reader, typo sleuth, artful editor, and for offering me sound advice, e.g., "Dad, this particular story is not fit for publication, ever." And to Joni Cole and the participants at her Writer's Center of WRJ who offered many insightful suggestions, lots of laughter, and overall encouragement regarding my work.

ABOUT THE AUTHOR

Will Wright lives, works, and plays in the Green Mountains of Vermont.

Cover design and artwork by Eric Wright

Illustrations by Kevin Wright

Printed in the USA
CPSIA information can be obtained
at www.ICGtesting.com
LVHW060809140124
768916LV00040B/1579